Llewellyn's
2019

Witches'
Spell-a-Day
Almanac

Holidays & Lore
Spells, Rituals & Meditations

Copyright 2018 Llewellyn Worldwide Ltd.
Cover Design: Kristi Carlson
Editing: Andrea Neff
Background photo: © PhotoDisc
Interior Art: © 2011, Steven McAfee
pp. 9, 29, 47, 69, 87, 105, 125, 145, 165, 187, 207, 225
Spell icons throughout: © 2011 Sherrie Thai

You can order Llewellyn books and annuals from *New Worlds*,
Llewellyn's catalog. To request a free copy of the catalog, call toll-free
1-877-NEW WRLD or visit our website at www.llewellyn.com.

ISBN: 978-0-7387-4617-3

Llewellyn is a registered trademark of Llewellyn Worldwide Ltd.
2143 Wooddale Drive
Woodbury, MN 55125

Printed in the United States of America

Contents

A Note on Magic and Spells 3

Spell-A-Day Icons 5

Spells at a Glance by Date and Category 6

2019 Year of Spells

       January 9

       February 29

       March 47

       April 69

       May 87

       June 105

       July 125

       August 145

       September 165

       October 187

       November 207

       December 225

Daily Magical Influences 247

Lunar Phases 247

Astrological Symbols 248

The Moon's Sign 249

Glossary of Magical Terms 250

About the Authors 252

A Note on Magic and Spells

The spells in the *Witches' Spell-A-Day Almanac* evoke everyday magic designed to improve our lives and homes. You needn't be an expert on magic to follow these simple rites and spells; as you will see if you use these spells throughout the year, magic, once mastered, is easy to perform. The only advanced technique required of you is the art of visualization.

Visualization is an act of controlled imagination. If you can call up in your mind a picture of your best friend's face or a flag flapping in the breeze, you can visualize. In magic, visualizations are used to direct and control magical energies. Basically the spellcaster creates a visual image of the spell's desired goal, whether it be perfect health, a safe house, or a protected pet.

Visualization is the basis of all good spells, and as such it is a tool that should be properly used. Visualization must be real in the mind of the spellcaster so it allows him or her to raise, concentrate, and send forth energy to accomplish the spell.

Perhaps when visualizing you'll find that you're doing everything right, but you don't feel anything. This is common, for we haven't been trained to acknowledge—let alone utilize—our magical abilities. Keep practicing, however, for your spells can "take" even if you're not the most experienced natural magician.

You will notice also that many spells in this collection have a some-what "light" tone. They are seemingly fun and frivolous, filled with rhyme and colloquial speech. This is not to diminish the seriousness of the purpose, but rather to create a relaxed atmosphere for the practitio-ner. Lightness of spirit helps focus energy; rhyme and common language help the spellcaster remember the words and train the mind where it is needed. The intent of this magic is indeed very serious at times, and magic is never to be trifled with.

Even when your spells are effective, magic won't usually sparkle before your very eyes. The test of magic's success is time, not immediate eye-popping results. But you can feel magic's energy for yourself by rubbing your palms together briskly for ten seconds, then holding them a few inches apart. Sense the energy passing through them, the warm tingle in your palms. This is the power raised and used in magic. It comes from within and is perfectly natural.

Among the features of the *Witches' Spell-A-Day Almanac* are an easy-to-use "book of days" format; new spells specifically tailored for each day

of the year (and its particular magical, astrological, and historical ener-gies); and additional tips and lore for various days throughout the year—including color correspondences based on planetary influences, obscure and forgotten holidays and festivals, and an incense of the day to help you waft magical energies from the ether into your space. Moon signs, phases, and voids are also included to help you find the perfect time for your rituals and spells. (All times in this book are Eastern Standard Time or Eastern Daylight Time.)

Enjoy your days, and have a magical year!

Spell—A—Day Icons

 New Moon

 Full Moon

 Abundance

 Altar

 Balance

 Clearing, Cleaning

 Garden

 Grab Bag

 Health, Healing

 Home

 Heart, Love

 Meditation, Divination

 Money, Prosperity

 Protection

 Relationship

 Success

 Travel, Communication

 Air Element

 Earth Element

 Fire Element

 Spirit Element

 Water Element

Spells at a Glance by Date and Category*

	Health, Healing	Protection	Success	Heart, Love	Clearing, Cleaning	Home	Meditation, Divination
Jan.	2, 11, 14, 18, 31	20	6		3, 13, 15, 17, 24, 26	1	7, 19, 28
Feb.	5	3, 12		8, 14, 23, 26	22, 28	1	2, 25, 28
March	3, 5, 16, 29	9, 15, 18, 19, 21		14			1
April	16			3	6, 9, 13, 27	25	7, 11, 17, 29
May	8	3, 27			25		
June	23	26		2, 4, 28		16	5
July	28	21		4	27	13	3, 7, 14, 22, 26, 30
Aug.	22	8, 19, 28		12, 20		1, 21, 27	
Sept.				12	9, 20, 22	6, 15	1, 10, 16, 17, 26
Oct.	5, 26	2, 19		1	22	21	
Nov.	14, 21			8, 23, 25	15, 24		3, 13
Dec.	7	14, 16		4		13, 15, 18	5, 10, 17, 19, 30, 31

*List is not comprehensive.

2019

Year of Spells

January

Happy New Year! The calendar year has begun and even though we may be in the depths of winter (in the Northern Hemisphere) or the height of summer (in the Southern Hemisphere), we stand at the threshold of fifty-two weeks filled with promise. Legend has it that this month is named to honor the Roman god Janus, a god of new beginnings and doorways, but it is also associated with Juno, the primary goddess of the Roman pantheon. Juno was said to be the protectress of the Roman Empire, and Janus (whose twin faces look to both the past and the future simultaneously) encourages new endeavors, transitions, and change in all forms. Since this month marks the beginning of the whole year, we can plant the seeds for long-term goals at this time, carefully plotting the course of our future success.

In the United States, there are three important holidays occurring in January: New Year's Day, Martin Luther King Jr. Day, and Inauguration Day. Each of these days exemplifies powerful change and transition. The dawn of a new year heralds a fresh start, and whether snow-covered or bathed in summer heat, January offers renewed possibilities for all.

Michael Furie

 January 1
Tuesday

4th ♏

☽ v/c 5:26 pm

Color of the Day: Scarlet
Incense of the Day: Geranium

New Year's Day – Kwanzaa ends

Bay Leaf Blessing

Happy New Year! Bless this new beginning by preparing a delicious stew or soup to warm the bellies and hearts of your friends and family. Add some magickal intentions for the coming year to the dish with bay leaves.

In folklore, the bay leaf is believed to grant wishes. In day-to-day use, it is a common kitchen herb, added to savory stews and soups while they simmer to add flavor. The bay leaf is removed prior to eating due to its fibrous texture.

Using a toothpick dipped in water, draw or write a wish on a bay leaf. A simple word is enough, such as *love*, *luck*, or *health*. Simmer the bay leaf in the stew as usual, and remove before serving. The symbol or word will have dissolved into the stew along with the intent behind it, spreading blessings to those who share your table.

Kate Freuler

January 2
Wednesday

4th ♏

☽ → ♐ 3:58 am

Color of the Day: Brown
Incense of the Day: Lilac

Beat the Blues Spell

For most of us, the holiday season is officially over. Like many of us, you've also probably been on a whirlwind schedule of holiday festivities since November. But now the holiday decorations come down and life returns to normal. So it's easy to feel blue at this time of year. Let this spell help you overcome the blues.

You'll need a cinnamon-scented candle, a sheet of pink construction paper, a red crayon, and a pen. First, light the candle and relax. Next, with the crayon draw a large heart on the paper. Inside the heart write this charm with the pen:

Season of goodwill and cheer,

Family, friends, and all
that I hold dear,

May you remain in my heart
throughout the year.

Let the candle burn out safely. Keep the paper in a special place. Read it when you need a lift. Remember to keep in touch with everyone who made your holidays special.

James Kambos

January 3
Thursday

4th ♐

Color of the Day: White
Incense of the Day: Nutmeg

The Waters of Purity (Simplified)

For this spell you will need your chalice filled with water.

Ground and center. Contemplate that which troubles you and imagine that it takes the form of a black smoke, which you now direct into the water with each exhale. Continue this until you feel the water has become dark and "poisoned." Enchant the water, saying:

Poison I have held within,

Fear or anger, shame or sin,

Transform by breath of witches' flame.

My power shines.

I here reclaim.

Take a cleansing breath and imagine breathing white fire directly into the water as you intone the sound of a low, vibrant hum. With each exhale, the darkness in the cup begins to transform in your mind's eye, becoming a brilliant crystalline luminescence. When you feel this is at its peak, reverently drink the water, feeling this light of transformation working its magic within you. Go about your day remembering this light within.

Storm Faerywolf

January 4
Friday

4th ♐

☽ v/c 12:41 pm
☽ → ♑ 1:55 pm

Color of the Day: Coral
Incense of the Day: Vanilla

The Number Four for a Balanced Beginning

Magic is often associated with the number three in witchcraft, but four can be a powerful magical number as well. Think of the four quarters, balanced and equal, for instance. In numerology, the number four signifies foundation and order, a practical approach to problems, and steady growth. What better way to start off the new year than to do a spell on the fourth day to tap into the magical power of four? Light four candles, one at a time, as you say this spell. (You can do this on the fourth of any month.)

Four the quarters, full of power,

Earth and air, fire and water.

Four the seasons, turning slowly,

Winter, spring, summer, fall.

Four for balance in my life,

Work and play, dark and light.

Four for a year filled with growth,

In measured pace, with joy for all.

Deborah Blake

January 5
Saturday

4th ♑

New Moon 8:28 pm

Color of the Day: Black
Incense of the Day: Sandalwood

Solar Eclipse

Bad habits, Fly Away!

A new moon and a solar eclipse: this is a time to welcome in and a time to banish. Such contradictions may seem impossible to resolve. The days begin to be longer, indicating an awakening, but we are in the time of the wheel of the year for introspection.

The first time you perform this casting, choose something simple, like a minor bad habit. Prepare your space, get comfortable, and envision your favorite bird. This friendly bird is awaiting your request. Next, envision the bad habit as well as the good habit that will replace it. After you write the bad habit on a piece of paper, your little bird puts out a leg and you tie the paper on. Fly away, bad habit! Now imagine that bird returning to you with the new good habit, or just the lack of the bad habit. Say:

Little bird of feathers and flight,

Take this bad habit and make it right.

Little bird of feathers and fun,

Bring me a good habit, now it is begun.

Emyme

 January 6
Sunday

1st ♑

Color of the Day: Gold
Incense of the Day: Frankincense

Stone Spell for Reaching Goals

Write your goal on a small slip of paper and fold it in half. Visualize yourself completing your goal—see yourself being successful. Place the paper on your altar or other special place and set a stone on top of the paper. Use either aqua aura quartz, aventurine, or a clear quartz crystal. As you put the stone in place, chant:

Success will come with motivation, planning, and determination.

Setting forth with heart and soul, I know I will achieve my goal.

Repeat this spell for each goal, each time seeing yourself achieving it successfully. Leave the stone and paper in place until you have achieved the goal. Let it serve as a reminder to keep working toward it.

Ember Grant

January 7
Monday

1st ♑

☽ v/c 1:20 am

☽ → ♒ 1:46 am

Color of the Day: Lavender
Incense of the Day: Neroli

All Is Well

We're a week into the new year. How's it going so far? While it can be hard to deal with change, it's best to remember that change is always with us. It's the way of the world!

If it's not too cold where you live, go outside early this morning and look around. See the rising sun and know there's always a new dawn. Look at the trees and imagine the tiny leaves curled up inside the branches. These leaves will awaken and unfurl. Look at your garden and imagine the fruits and veggies sleeping under the earth (and maybe under snow) and know that they will stretch and rise and bloom.

Back inside, sit quietly and meditate with this paraphrase of the words of the medieval English mystic Dame Julian of Norwich:

All is well.

All things are well.

All manner of things are well.

All can only be well.

Barbara Ardinger

January 8
Tuesday

1st ♒

Color of the Day: Red
Incense of the Day: Cedar

Star Light, Star Bright

Winter skies are exceptionally clear. The cold air keeps pollutants at bay and gives us the opportunity to gaze at the stars, unparalleled in other seasons.

Science teaches that the starlight we see comes from stars that may have burnt out many light years ago.

But does that really matter? Perhaps it would if you were a scientist, but most of us are not astronomers. We simply appreciate the ability to be awed by the beautiful night sky.

An old children's rhyme reads:

Star light, star bright,

The first star I see tonight;

I wish I may, I wish I might,

Have the wish I wish tonight.

What could be more perfect than the sincere wish of a child?

Tonight, stand beneath the winter sky and find a star that calls to you. Close your eyes and make a wish. May all your wishes come true.

Najah Lightfoot

 # January 9
Wednesday

1st ≈

☽ v/c 11:53 am

☽ → ♓ 2:44 pm

Color of the Day: White
Incense of the Day: Bay laurel

Spell for Stability

Choose four rocks that appeal to you. Hold each one in your hands individually as you focus your thoughts on something that helps you feel secure and grounded. You might think of family, wealth, shelter, love, health, or other concepts. As you hold each rock, imagine that you have an abundance of whatever that rock represents. Conjure up the emotions of security and project these feelings into each rock. Place the rocks at each corner of your property, or hide them near the corners of a room where a stabilizing force is most needed. This spell will help settle erratic energies to bring a grounded, centering energy to your home.

Melanie Marquis

January 10
Thursday

1st ♓

Color of the Day: Purple
Incense of the Day: Carnation

Soul-Baring Spell

The Sumerian goddess Inanna's birth was celebrated in early January. In an early descent myth, Inanna journeyed to the underworld, stripping away her armor and clothing at seven points during her descent. Baring herself, Inanna faced illness, grief, loss, regret, and death, seeing them as part of the great wheel of life.

Invoke Inanna. Bare your soul. Dispel your worries. Seven times, let your mind rest on your troubles, whispering:

Inanna, brave warrior, please be near,

Walk with me through ____ and fear.

Stripped of worry and deep-held dread,

I face life bare, open, and ready instead.

With each whisper, symbolically remove a piece of clothing or jewelry. When you are naked, know that, like Inanna, you must face whatever life brings. As you put your clothes back on, understand that facing your fears enables you to survive them. It is all part of the cycle of the wheel of life.

Dallas Jennifer Cobb

January 11
Friday

1st ♓

☽ v/c 9:25 am

Color of the Day: Pink
Incense of the Day: Cypress

A Dab Will Do Vanilla Spell

Those who work the standard business week look forward to Fridays as the end of the work week. We all hope for a pleasant and smooth Friday. Vanilla resonates with Friday's energies, and its scent is known to have a calming effect and improve the mood. Making ourselves and those around us calmer can't be a bad thing. So with the aim to end the week on a pleasant note, put on a couple dabs of vanilla extract or essential oil, take three deep breaths in and out, and then say to yourself:

Vanilla, sweet and relaxing,

Help make the day less taxing.

Unwind and calm,

*For any sore mood you
are a soothing balm.*

May all our cares float away.

To all a pleasant Friday!

Blake Octavian Blair

January 12
Saturday

1st ♓

☽ → ♈ 3:18 am

Color of the Day: Blue
Incense of the Day: Patchouli

Frigg Altar and Ritual

Frigg is an important Norse goddess, emblematic of the northern housewife. Her domain includes love, fertility, marriage, domesticity, destiny, and protection. Today, set aside time to honor Frigg.

Altar

In the bathroom, set out a silvery cloth, roses in a vase of water, a censer, and a skein of sky-blue yarn. Light some charcoals in the censer. Sprinkle with sandalwood chips— an incense for remembrance.

Ritual

1. Take a shower, using soap containing birch essential oil.

2. Clarify your thoughts with sips of feverfew tea.

3. Wear a white robe (dress). Cinch the waist with gold cord from which keys hang, repre- senting silence and forgetfulness.

4. Pin feathers in your hair, forming a crown. (Colors: white, gray, or green.)

5. Go outside. Look up toward the clouds of Asgard (Frigg's home).

6. Spin clockwise, visualizing your yarn in the clouds. Envision them holding keys to your life, home, and happiness.

7. Stop briefly.

8. Spin counterclockwise.

9. Recite:

*Praise Frigg! Show me the future.
Help me fulfill my destiny.*

Blessed be!

Stephanie Rose Bird

January 13
Sunday

1st ♈

Color of the Day: Yellow
Incense of the Day: Almond

Blockbuster Spell

Chances are you have experienced some resistance making those New Year's resolutions happen. Cast this spell when you need to bust through the blocks between you and manifestation.

Combine three pinches each of lemon zest, red pepper, mint, allspice, and hyssop, then mix well. Dress a red candle with dragon's blood oil and then roll in the herb mix. In a fire-safe dish, burn this candle at dusk while facing the west and say:

Five cleansing herbs come to my aid,
with the sixth, the path is laid.

Six allies take my hand,
the seventh, here I stand.

With these spirits I blow apart,
all that would deny me start.

Blockbuster candle open the way,
unblock my future like night and day.

Let the candle burn out completely and safely and bury any remnants.

Devin Hunter

January 14
Monday

1st ♈

2nd Quarter 1:46 am

☽ v/c 10:56 am

☽ → ♉ 1:31 pm

Color of the Day: Gray
Incense of the Day: Narcissus

Pu'er to the Rescue

It seems that there is always a screen, television, or hologram drawing our attention, leaving our vision more exhausted that we might realize. When your eyes have simply decoded too much light and information, try this soothing tea for ocular health and healing.

Fill two paper tea bags, one for each eye, with the following measure in each bag:

- 1 teaspoon Pu'er aged Chinese black tea, freshly crushed
- ¼ teaspoon eyebright leaves and flowers
- 1 teaspoon dehydrated cucumber flakes
- 1 teaspoon sesame seeds, freshly crushed
- 1 teaspoon quinoa seeds, freshly crushed
- ¼ teaspoon ginseng extract

In two separate cups, steep for five minutes. Let the bags cool on a plate. When warm to the touch, place them over your closed eyes. Lie back and relax, sipping this potent antioxidant brew. It will invigorate blood flow and improve your vision while it reduces the signs of fine lines and wrinkles. Enjoy.

Estha McNevin

January 15
Tuesday

2nd ♉

Color of the Day: Black
Incense of the Day: Basil

Cool Down Spell

This is a ritual bath for when you are plagued by anger or negativity.

Go outside and make a snowball with your hands. As you pack the snow together in the shape of a ball, charge it with the ability to vanquish or banish energy. See it pulsing with pure white cleansing light, and feel its cold clarity in your hands.

Immediately, go draw yourself a warm bath. Get in the bath, hold the snowball over you, and say:

Pure white light, pure white snow,

Extinguish this anger, make it go!

Drop the snowball into the water. (A jar of rain can be substituted for a snowball.) As it melts and cools the water around your body, feel it also cooling the coals of your ire. See it transform your aura from angry dark red to calm blue.

Kate Freuler

January 16
Wednesday

2nd ♉

☽ v/c 1:34 pm

☽ → ♊ 8:00 pm

Color of the Day: Topaz
Incense of the Day: Marjoram

Triple Circle Money Spell

For this spell you will need the following materials:

- A pen and paper
- Patchouli oil
- A green candle and holder
- Several coins
- Chamomile flowers
- Sea salt

Ground and center. On the paper, draw a symbol for money, such as a dollar sign, and the specific amount you are looking for. With the oil, anoint the four corners of the paper, along with the center. Place the paper on the center of your altar. Oil the candle, put it in the holder, and place it on the center of the paper. Surround it with a circle made from the coins, then encircle all of that with the chamomile flowers. Encircle this all with salt.

Light the candle, saying:

Flame of candle, sign of money,

Herb of riches, salt of earth,

By these signs, these coins, I conjure.

In triple circle fortune shines.

Let the candle burn down safely, then burn the paper. Take a bath with the salt and chamomile. Spend the coins. The money will come.

Storm Faerywolf

January 17
Thursday

2nd ♊

Color of the Day: Crimson
Incense of the Day: Apricot

Ditch Witching

Today is Ditch New Year's Resolutions Day. Maybe you're succeeding with all yours, in which case, keep up the good work. But most of us have at least one resolution that isn't working out. Those become a burden and a nagging source of guilt. So today is the day to assess your progress and decide which resolutions to ditch. You can always try again another time.

For this spell, you need a small piece of scrap paper and a pencil. It's a great idea to pick up a piece of paper litter to write on, like a newspaper. Write down your resolution(s) to ditch. Concentrate on the weight, and then shrug it off. This is no longer a current goal; you can spend your energy on something else now.

Take the paper to a ditch and throw it in. Bury it if you wish. Walk away without looking back.

Elizabeth Barrette

January 18
Friday

2nd ♊

☽ v/c 8:32 pm
☽ → ♋ 10:44 pm

Color of the Day: Coral
Incense of the Day: Alder

Lose Weight Spell

If all the food you ate over the holidays has caught up with you and has settled on your hips or stomach, this spell may help your diet plan. First, pick a sensible diet plan to help you lose the extra weight. Now you may begin the spell.

You'll need a sheet of plain white paper, a marker, and a pair of scissors. Using the marker, draw an image of how you think you look now. Cut out the image. Place it where you'll see it every day. When you lose some weight, take the scissors and trim a little off the image, and say:

Layer by layer, off the weight will peel.
Soon, a new me shall be revealed.

Repeat this every time you lose more weight. Throw away the scraps you cut off immediately. Just keep focusing on your image getting smaller until you reach your goal.

James Kambos

January 19
Saturday

2nd ♋

Color of the Day: Indigo
Incense of the Day: Magnolia

Darkness Divination

The dark, cold nights of winter can seem long and tiresome, but don't forget that the quiet, slower pace of this season can be useful, too. It is a good time to look inward, to go deeper. In short, it is a great time for divination.

Take advantage of the quiet and you might hear the answers to questions you didn't even know you were asking. If you are comfortable with tarot cards or rune stones, you can use those. Otherwise, you can light a black or white candle and gaze into a dark-colored bowl filled with water. Ask: *What do I need to know?* Then say this spell and pull a few cards or stones or look into the water to see if an image appears:

Darkness, darkness, of the night,

Show some answers to my sight.

Deborah Blake

 January 20
Sunday

2nd ♋

☉ → ♒ 4:00 am

☽ v/c 8:50 pm

☽ → ♌ 10:54 pm

Color of the Day: Orange
Incense of the Day: Heliotrope

Blessing for a Book of Shadows

Use this spell to bless and protect your Book of Shadows, keeping it a safe and secure place to record your thoughts, secrets, spells, and recipes. These books often take the form of personal journals for some people, and they deserve to be well cared for. It doesn't matter if your "book" is a journal, a binder, or even a digital file.

Place the book (in whatever form it takes) on your altar with a candle on each side. Be careful not to singe the edges or melt it. Visualize your book as a sacred repository for all your magic. Chant:

All my thoughts and all my spells,
bless them and protect them well.

Cover to cover and page to page,
preserve these words for any age.

Ember Grant

January 21
Monday

2nd ♌

🌕 **Full Moon** 12:16 am

Color of the Day: White
Incense of the Day: Clary sage

Martin Luther King Jr. Day – Lunar Eclipse

What Is Your Dream?

Today we celebrate the work of Dr. Martin Luther King Jr. Go to YouTube and watch his "I Have a Dream" speech, which he delivered on August 28, 1963, during the March on Washington.

What dream do you have? Cast your circle and set up your altar with four green candles and symbols of what can make your dream come true. Light the candles, call in the four quarters, and invoke the god or goddess who can send the elements of your dream to you. Speak this invocation:

I dream, and dreams come true.

I dream and make my life anew.

Now speak your dream aloud. Describe it in the minutest detail. Take as much time as necessary so the Invisibles know precisely what you want. Speak the invocation again. Remember that Dr. King's dream has not yet come true, though, well, it's moving along. Like his, your dream will probably arrive incrementally.

Barbara Ardinger

January 22
Tuesday

3rd ♌

☽ v/c 8:19 pm

☽ → ♍ 10:22 pm

Color of the Day: Maroon
Incense of the Day: Ylang-ylang

Answer Cat's Questions Day

Here is a fun little experiment for this day. For those of you who have cats as pets and/or familiars, let today be Answer Cat's Questions Day. One of my cats literally answers one specific question: when I ask (in a sing-song catlike voice) *Where are you?* Stars always answers *Right here!* in her sing-song cat voice. Now, who knows if she knows what is being asked or if she is really answering, but seeing as we always partake in this ritual around feeding time—well, I think it's safe to say we both know what is being asked and answered.

Just for fun, try this game. Sit with your cat(s) and tell them out loud that you will answer any questions they have. See what happens and write down the results. Say:

My furry friend, my special companion,

What questions do you have for me?

Help me understand, I will do my best,

And give you answers happily.

Emyme

 ## January 23
Wednesday

3rd ♏

Color of the Day: Yellow
Incense of the Day: Honeysuckle

Silence Is Golden

The holidays are over. The boxes, baubles, and ribbons have been put away. On this day of the week dedicated to Mercury, arise early, silence your phone, and leave your headphones at home. Bundle up and go for a walk.

Resist the temptation to speak or talk out loud. If you live in a winter climate, breathe in the crisp January air. If you live in a southern climate, notice the awakening of birds and green trees. Walk softly. Ease your breathing and merge with the natural world.

When you feel ready to return home, do so. Once you get home, take a moment to write down any impressions, images, messages, or thoughts that came to you on your walk.

Practice and repeat this ritual as necessary. Magick is always afoot, waiting and willing to share with us if we will only take time to listen and be with it.

Najah Lightfoot

January 24
Thursday

3rd ♏

☽ v/c 8:50 am
☽ → ♎ 11:02 pm

Color of the Day: Green
Incense of the Day: Balsam

Spell for Relieving Stress

Do this spell to lessen stress when you have a pile of chores that can't be put off any longer. Stand before your sink of dirty dishes or pile of dirty laundry and envision your stressful energies flowing out of your hands and into the piles or stacks of things in need of a good washing. Touch the dishes or dirty clothes and say to the universe that it is your stress that you will be washing away today. Think about how just as clothes and dishes get dirty but can be cleaned to look brand-new, so too can you wash away the accumulated stresses of the day to find yourself renewed and refreshed. As you proceed with your chore, imagine that you are washing away your stress as the water rushes over your laundry or as you scrub your dishes.

Melanie Marquis

 ## January 25
Friday

3rd ♎

Color of the Day: Purple
Incense of the Day: Orchid

Being Venusian

Friday is ruled by the goddess and the planet Venus, which corresponds with peace, agreements, cooperation, fertility, joy, love, and good fortune but also jealousy, strife, and promiscuity. Relationships evoke intense energy, and while we wish for the best, sometimes they bring out the worst. Being human means we can exercise free will. So today, consciously choose to manifest the higher vibration of Venus in relationships.

Venus's colors are pink, green, and turquoise. Choose a garment of clothing in one of these colors, and as you put on the garment, consciously robe yourself in Venusian energy. Slide into that t-shirt and wear your passion. Put on the pants of engaged and loyal relations. Slip into a dress for joyful dancing. Then chant:

In Venusian magic I am cloaked,

To honor my relations I invoke

Joy and love and cooperation.

Today I increase my good fortune.

I am Venusian.

So be it.

Dallas Jennifer Cobb

 ## January 26
Saturday

3rd ♎
☽ v/c 12:21 am
☽ → ♏ 2:31 am
4th Quarter 4:10 pm

Color of the Day: Yellow
Incense of the Day: Marigold

Moon in Libra Sanctuary Spell

Today the moon is in Libra, bringing about a deep need for peace and harmony in our lives. There is perhaps nothing more important than the home being a sanctuary, so today and whenever you might have need, cast this spell to ensure that peaceful and harmonious energies reside in your home.

Anoint a white candle with hyssop oil and place it in a fire-safe dish somewhere central in your home. Light the candle and say:

Make peace my right and end the fight to live without regret.

Let peace be here to shed the fear, subdue the greatest threat.

Clean your home as thoroughly as possible. At the very least, spend some time picking up the clutter and organizing the chaos until you feel the energy shift in your space. Allow the candle to burn out completely and safely.

Devin Hunter

 # January 27
Sunday

3rd ♎

Color of the Day: Gray
Incense of the Day: Ivy

Aquarian Bedside Altar

Today, set aside time to devote to Aquarius by building a bedside altar.

Begin by charging a piece of amethyst. This stone helps people express their feelings and brings forth good communication. Soak the amethyst in a glass bowl of rainwater.

Set out an aluminum sheet pan or cover your table in aluminum foil. Place a pot of orchids on the aluminum. This is your reminder to reflect on fertility and creativity and to always be curious. Orchid is a flower of love, luxury, beauty, strength, and virility.

Light a beautiful aquamarine candle, with a fresh ocean scent.

Add the bowl of rainwater containing the amethyst to your altar.

Reflect on the purifying and strengthening qualities of this Aquarian altar before you go to sleep. Snuff out the candle.

Your Aquarian bedside altar is designed to nurture fertility in thought and deed, spark innovation, and feed your curiosity.

Stephanie Rose Bird

January 28
Monday

4th ♏
☽ v/c 5:39 pm

Color of the Day: Ivory
Incense of the Day: Hyssop

Cosmos Contemplation to honor the Challenger

On this date in 1986, the US space shuttle Challenger exploded shortly after takeoff, claiming the lives of all onboard. These men and women lost their lives in pursuit of greater knowledge of the cosmos we exist in.

This evening, go outside, look up at the sky, and contemplate the vastness and mystery of the cosmos. Contemplate how we are only a small part in the vastness, how much we have learned and how much we have yet to learn. Pay attention to the stars. Are any particular constellations visible to you? What message might they be sending to you as they grace you with their presence?

Spend as much time in meditation as you desire. When you're finished, leave a small earth-friendly offering outdoors. When returning indoors, light a candle and say a prayer of remembrance on your altar for the crew of the Challenger.

Blake Octavian Blair

January 29
Tuesday

4th ♏

☽ → ♐ 9:33 am

Color of the Day: Gray
Incense of the Day: Ginger

Success Spell

For this spell you will need the following items:

- 1 spool of white thread
- 1 needle
- 1 white emergency/blackout candle
- 1 sharp yellow stone or rugged glass bead
- 1 lock of your own hair

Sitting in a sunny location, begin the spell in the early afternoon. Take your measure by cutting a piece of the thread and measuring from the center of your head to the bottom of your feet. Threading the needle puts the energy of your spirit into the thread.

Contemplate one single goal. Picture all of the stages of work ahead. Pass the needle through the middle of the candle so the ends of the thread dangle out of either side. Then thread the stone or bead onto the string on the right side of the candle. Tie your hair to the string on the left side, and bind the two ends together in a triple knot as you cast your intention. Burn the candle today as an offering to the sun and set your goals within sight of the new year ahead.

Estha McNevin

 January 30
Wednesday

4th ♐

Color of the Day: Brown
Incense of the Day: Lavender

Keep the Wheels Turning

Most of modern society relies on technology, yet it gets little mention in magic. Our ancestors worshipped aspects of what was modern technology to them, such as smithcraft. Here, then, is a spell to beseech the spirit of technology for smooth functioning.

To cast this spell, you'll need a representation of a wheel. It can be as simple as a picture or as fancy as fidget jewelry with wheels that actually turn. Visualize your wheel as a personification of technology. Touch the wheel to three working machines of importance to you, perhaps your car, refrigerator, and computer. Give thanks to the spirit of technology for what you have. Ask it to keep everything in your life running as it should.

Afterward, keep the wheel in a safe place. If it's a picture, you can keep it on your altar. Jewelry may be worn or stored in a jewelry box.

Elizabeth Barrette

January 31
Thursday

4th ♐
☽ v/c 5:33 pm
☽ → ♑ 7:47 pm

Color of the Day: Turquoise
Incense of the Day: Mulberry

Healing Light Candle Spell

Carve an image of the sun into a yellow (or white) votive candle. Anoint the candle with eucalyptus or rosemary oil, if you have it. As you light the candle, visualize healing light, like beams of sunshine, streaming and flowing into you (or into someone who needs healing energy). See the light touching every part of the body, dissolving any trace of illness and restoring wellness.

Chant the following spell. If necessary, replace "me" with the name of the person who needs to receive the energy.

Healing light, light of love,

Fill me with your rays.

Renew, restore, and burn away

All illness with your blaze.

Healing fire, fire of love,

Let your flames devour

Every trace of malady—

Send me strength and power.

Allow the candle to burn out safely. Repeat as desired.

Ember Grant

February

The word *February* is based on the Latin *februa* and refers to the Roman festival of purification of the same name. This festival later became integrated with February's infamous Lupercalia. Since ancient times, February has been observed as a month of cleansing, cleaning, purification, and preparation for the warm months ahead. We see the Celtic Imbolg (Candlemas) celebrated in February to perpetuate the summoning of solar light. In many parts of the world at this time, the promise of sunlight seems bleak, even imaginary. The world around us is slowly awakening from its wintery slumber, and some semblance of excitement begins to grow in the hearts of those attuned to the seasonal tides.

Daylight hours are short in February, so this time of year can sometimes feel depressive. We must actively cultivate our inner light through regular exercise, solid sleep, meditation, yoga, ritual, studying, artwork, and planning ahead for the year. When performing magickal work this month, remember that your energy levels may be lower than usual and you must summon your own inner light to strengthen and illuminate your efforts. Do whatever it takes to stay on top of your game, keep energized, cultivate happiness, and embrace February's cleansing rebirth!

Raven Digitalis

February 1
Friday

4th ♍

Color of the Day: Pink
Incense of the Day: Yarrow

Out with the Old Spell

According to tradition, this was the last day holiday greenery was allowed in the home or church. To leave it up after this date was believed to bring misfortune. Keeping this in mind, this is a good day to freshen up your home. Remove any clutter and discard items you no longer need. If you have any sickly houseplants, replace them. If your budget allows, buy some decorative items. Pillows for the sofa or a cozy throw are good ideas. In the evening, light an orange candle. Gaze at the flame and say:

*Divine Power, everything is
fresh, the old is gone.*

Bless my home and prepare me

For spring and the shining sun.

Watch the candle flame and visualize the strengthening sun blessing you with good fortune. Let the candle burn out in a safe place.

James Kambos

 ## February 2
Saturday

4th ♍

Color of the Day: Blue
Incense of the Day: Rue

Imbolc – Groundhog Day

Divining Spring

For this spell you will need a white candle and a yellow rose. It is traditional on this day to perform divination focused on the end of winter and the emergence of spring. On Imbolc morning, about one to two hours before midday, go outside and recite the following cantrip:

If Imbolc day is bright and clear,

Then winter lingers cold and near.

If Imbolc day is overcast,

Then early spring shall come at last.

Meditate on your environment. Pay attention to the temperature, the sounds, the light, etc. Tune in to the natural rhythms of the land around you. If it is sunny, then winter will linger. If it is cloudy, then spring will soon come. Return inside and light the white candle in front of a vase holding the yellow rose as a blessing of winter moving into spring.

Storm Faerywolf

February 3
Sunday

4th ♑

☽ v/c 5:53 am
☽ → ♒ 8:03 am

Color of the Day: Amber
Incense of the Day: Eucalyptus

Setsubun-sai Bean-Throwing Ceremony

According to Shinto belief, today is when the spirit world is closest to ours. In Japan, bean throwing is a popular way to mark the end of winter and the eve of the first day of spring. The idea is to employ the mystical powers of beans to scare away evil and usher in goodness. Involve everyone in your home in this ceremony.

First, you need one person to be an ogre, to symbolize evil. An ogre toy or mask or a face painted like that of an ogre will work.

Next, select roasted soybeans with a flavor profile you prefer. Dry-roasted nuts are very healthy. They can be salty or spicy in flavor.

Toss seven soybeans at the ogre. The ogre runs away.

Then each participant eats the number of beans that represents their age.

Stephanie Rose Bird

February 4
Monday

4th ♒

🌑 New Moon 4:04 pm

Color of the Day: Silver
Incense of the Day: Lily

Spell for Youthfulness

Use this new moon spell to help you retain a youthful glow. Place a round mirror outside at night to catch the rays of the new moon's light. Be sure that the mirror is clean and free of any smudges or fingerprints. Retrieve the mirror before moonset and gaze into it so that you can see both your face and the moon reflected in the glassy surface. Envision your face being flooded with moonlight, erasing any impurities and smoothing any wrinkles or rough patches. Say into the mirror:

I am beautiful like the moon, born again and born anew! Rays of moon and starry sky, put a twinkle in my eye!

Smile into the mirror to complete the spell. Keep this mirror out of the sunlight and gaze into it only at nighttime to give yourself a boost of beauty and freshness.

Melanie Marquis

February 5
Tuesday

1st ♒

☽ v/c 6:59 pm

☽ → ♓ 9:02 pm

Color of the Day: Scarlet
Incense of the Day: Cedar

Lunar New Year (Pig)

Manifesting happiness

Today is Lunar New Year in China, Japan, Vietnam, Korea, Mongolia, and Tibet, and 2019 is the year of the Earth Pig. The last animal in the Chinese zodiac, Pig is compassionate, generous, and diligent. Earth pig is communicative and popular among friends. Today, set an intention to cultivate happiness from within.

Envision yourself happy from within. What do you look like? Feel like? How are you changed?

Now that you are not dependent on outside stuff or people, ask:

What within me brings me happiness?

Write it down. For the next fourteen days, devote a few moments daily to cultivating these qualities of character or these personal practices. Let happiness from within grow with the waxing moon and set the tone for the year to come.

Dallas Jennifer Cobb

February 6
Wednesday

1st ♓

Color of the Day: Topaz
Incense of the Day: Bay laurel

Messages from Reindeer

Today is Sami National Day, a day of celebration in Norway for the Sami people. These shamanic people are renowned for their connection to reindeer. The Sami are famous reindeer herders. Reindeer are also used to pull sleighs, and the Sami culture holds Reindeer as a spirit of great power. All parts of deceased reindeer are used for practical and sacred purposes and treated with reverence. There are many hypotheses that Santa's sleigh being depicted as driven by reindeer may have roots in Sami shamans' multifaceted relationship with reindeer.

Perhaps the spirit of Reindeer holds a message for you too. Create sacred space according to your tradition, and enter a state of altered consciousness, either through shamanic journeying or meditation. Visit the spirit of Reindeer. Ask it what wisdom it has to share with you. Journal on your experiences.

Blake Octavian Blair

february 7
Thursday

1st ♓

☽ v/c 5:14 pm

Color of the Day: Purple
Incense of the Day: Jasmine

Feel the Rhythm

On this day in 1964, the Beatles landed for the first time in the United States. Their arrival is legendary. When the feet of those four young men touched US soil, a shock wave was sent across the world that is still going. The Beatles' music and style set off rhythms and pulses of love that resonated deeply with our souls and intentions for a better world.

Today, grab your favorite drum, tambourine, or rattle. If you have none of these, clap your hands. Bang on your drum, shake your rattle or tambourine, or clap your hands, slowly at first, then faster and faster, until you can feel the beat in your soul. When the rhythm reaches a crescendo, let loose a whoop or a holler. Know you are energetically connected to the rhythms of the universe. Know you are a rhythm that can send good vibrations across the world.

Najah Lightfoot

 ## february 8
Friday

1st ♓

☽ → ♈ 9:34 am

Color of the Day: White
Incense of the Day: Mint

Creative Romance Month

Everyone knows about Valentine's Day, but February is also Creative Romance Month. This can mean spicing up a current relationship, seeking a new one, or celebrating things like platonic romance.

This spell requires hearts, such as beads or chocolates, one for you and one for your partner(s). Use red for sexual romance or pink for platonic. Hold your heart and imagine what you have to give. Hold your partner's heart and focus on what you wish to receive. If you have some current partner(s), give your heart to them and keep theirs on your altar. If not, you can leave yours in a public place such as a park to signify your openness to new relationships.

In any case, take time today to do sweet and quirky things for people you love, whether the relationship is erotic or not. Affectionate gestures increase the amount of love in your life.

Elizabeth Barrette

February 9
Saturday

1st ♈

Color of the Day: Brown
Incense of the Day: Pine

Ice Lolly Spell

In these dark months we really start to miss the power of the sun. This edible spell draws upon solar energy, reminds us of summer, and is a tasty treat all in one.

For this spell you will need ice lolly (Popsicle) sticks, reusable ice lolly molds, and orange juice.

On each ice lolly stick, use washable nontoxic marker to write a goal, such as love, prosperity, or friendship. Place one stick in each ice lolly mold. Set the orange juice in direct sunlight for a moment or two, charging it with the warm, illuminating, joyful energy of the sun. Fill the lolly molds with the juice, then place in the freezer overnight. Each lolly will absorb the intent of the goal written on the stick.

As you eat the frozen treats, take into yourself the power to achieve your goals, boosted by solar energy.

Kate Freuler

February 10
Sunday

1st ♈

☽ v/c 6:48 pm
☽ → ♉ 8:28 pm

Color of the Day: Orange
Incense of the Day: Hyacinth

The Parking Space Word

I've received fan email for this spell, which I've published in various places, including earlier almanacs, so I'm repeating it this year. No matter where we live, if we drive a car, we need to park it somewhere. Whether we're at work or at the mall or at home in an urban neighborhood that has more multi-family dwellings than there are parking spaces, we need to park our car.

Speak the Parking Space Word:

ZZZZZAAAAAAZZZZZ.

Speak it loud and with great energy. It seems to work best if you plan ahead and say where you want to park. Speak the Word, therefore, when you turn a corner or enter the parking lot:

ZZZZZAAAAAZZZZZ.
Parking space at_____.

Be aware that the Word doesn't always work immediately. Sometimes you have to drive around the block or around the lot. Repeat the Word every time you turn a corner. It will work.

Barbara Ardinger

February 11
Monday

1st ♉

Color of the Day: Gray
Incense of the Day: Narcissus

Get Out Your Guitar Day

For those of you lucky enough to own a guitar, today is the day to get it out and put it to use. Clean and tune. Strum and stroke. It's a Monday, so play some Monday blues or some music to make Monday bearable. Minerva and Apollo are said to be the patrons of music, and Saint Cecilia is often depicted with a stringed instrument. Choose one deity to honor and light a candle or stick of incense as you play. Offer up gratitude for your musical ability. When you are done, put the guitar away with care and dignity. For those not so blessed with talent? Try one of the music streaming sources—find a station of guitar music of any kind to suit your mood (classical, Spanish, jazz, blues, rock), light some candles, and settle in. Music soothes the savage breast. Your soul will be better for it. Say:

> Music soothes me, energizes
> me, enters me.
>
> Make me whole, inspire
> and cleanse me.
>
> Notes float into the universe
> for all to heal.

Emyme

February 12
Tuesday

1st ♉

☽ v/c 5:26 pm
2nd Quarter 5:26 pm

Color of the Day: Red
Incense of the Day: Bayberry

Herbal Protection Amulet

To make a protection amulet using herbs, gather one acorn and a pinch of as many of the following herbs as you can: parsley, basil, cedar, sage, and valerian. Place the items in a small white or red drawstring bag (or sew your own bundle). Place the amulet in a circle of white tealights and, as the candles are burning, visualize your specific protection needs. Chant:

> I ask these plants with much respect
> to guard, defend me and protect—
> keep harm away, ill will at bay,
> let misfortune hold no sway.

When all the candles have burned out safely, remove the amulet and carry it with you.

Ember Grant

February 13
Wednesday

2nd ♉

☽ → ♊ 4:32 am

Color of the Day: Brown
Incense of the Day: Lilac

A Mighty Dead Offering

Today we mark the passing of Gerald Gardner (1884–1964), the father of Wicca, and ask his spirit for guidance and blessing as one of the Mighty Dead.

For this spell you will need these materials:

- An image of Gerald Gardner

- A black candle and holder

- Some anointing oil for the Mighty Dead (such as that which contains anise)

- An offering bowl and cup

- A food item and beverage of your choosing

Arrange your altar with the image in the center. Dress the candle (rub the oil on it) and empower it for the Mighty Dead, then place in the holder before the photo. Before all of this place the empty offering bowl and cup.

Ground and center. Focus on the photo. Light the candle. Say:

Gerald Gardner of the Mighty Dead,

Accept this offering and strengthen the thread:

The lineage of the magic blood

That guides me on the witch's road.

Place your offerings in the bowl and cup and share in the "feast."

Storm Faerywolf

February 14
Thursday

2nd ♊

Color of the Day: Green
Incense of the Day: Myrrh

Valentine's Day

A Love Spell for Everyone

Today is widely celebrated as Valentine's Day, a holiday dedicated to love. If you are alone or if things aren't going well in your relationship, you might be tempted to cast a love spell. But such things can be tricky and interfere with free will. Instead, try casting a spell to bring more love into your life in all the positive ways the universe might send you. We can all use more love, right? If you want, you can light a red or pink candle while you say this spell:

God and Goddess up above,

Send to me the gift of love.

On this day and all that follow,

Fill with love all spaces hollow.

Let my heart be filled with light,

And send me all the love that's right.

Deborah Blake

February 15
Friday

2nd ♊

☽ v/c 7:48 am
☽ → ♋ 9:03 am

Color of the Day: Rose
Incense of the Day: Rose

Spell for honest and Wise Communication

Use this spell when communication patterns have become stale, negative, limited, or dishonest. Write your name and the name of the person with whom you wish to communicate on two separate pieces of paper. Fill a clean, clear jar with salt and a handful of dried or fresh sage leaves. Place the two papers inside the jar. Don't put a lid on it; leave it open. Gently swirl the contents of the jar until the papers are completely submerged in the salt and sage as you envision yourself having a productive, wise, and honest conversation with the person in question. Leave the jar in the area where you're most likely to come into contact with the person, or alternatively, take out the two slips of paper, fold them together, and keep this tucked inside your pocket during conversations.

Melanie Marquis

February 16
Saturday

2nd ♋

Color of the Day: Black
Incense of the Day: Sage

Spirit Guide Budget Blessing

Congratulations! You have officially made it through the holidays and can now take a look at your family and personal financial goals. Sit down today and spend some time reviewing your financial documents, taking inventory of how well you feel you are able to make ends meet, how well you are able to save for bigger and better things, and how you are freeing yourself of financial burden when possible.

Taking this information, meditate and ask your guides for information they might have about the way you spend and save money and then ask them to help you create or adjust your budget. Write out this budget on paper, making sure to have a savings goal in mind, and post it someplace where it will be seen regularly. Call upon your guides each time you see it to help you make empowered financial decisions and stick to your budget.

Devin Hunter

February 17
Sunday

2nd ♋

☽ v/c 9:17 am
☽ → ♌ 10:21 am

Color of the Day: Yellow
Incense of the Day: Juniper

Fornacalia Movable Feast

Fornacalia is a movable feast in honor of Fornax, goddess of the furnace, oven, and kiln. This fire goddess is also related to bread making. We celebrate her in thanksgiving for the earliest, newly gathered grain crops.

Create a fire outdoors, perhaps in a barbeque pit or in some other safe manner.

In a ceramic bowl or jar, place some spelt.

Have your group gather in a circle around the fire. Call the directions together:

Spirits of the north, we welcome you!

Spirits of the east, we welcome you!

Spirits of the south, we welcome you!

Spirits of the west, we welcome you!

The leader says:

Goddess of the hearth!

The group repeats:

Goddess of the hearth!

The leader throws a handful of spelt toward the heavens.

The group duplicates these actions.

The circle is closed.

The group breaks bread together. Corn bread or some other grainy loaf is shared with everyone seated in a circle.

Stephanie Rose Bird

February 18
Monday

2nd ♌

☉ → ♓ 6:04 pm

Color of the Day: Lavender
Incense of the Day: Neroli

Presidents' Day

Chakra Check-Up

It may not seem like an odd number would have much to do with balance; however, the number seven is a perfect number for balance. Generally, we recognize that we have seven main chakras, and that for optimum spiritual balance, we aim to keep our chakras aligned and in balance with each other.

Today is a great day to work with your chakras, as it is the forty-ninth day of the year, seven multiplied by itself. Find or make a simple pendulum, and use it to check your chakras. First smudge or otherwise clear your pendulum. Then place it over each chakra, one at a time, and see if it spins clockwise (indicating balance) or counterclockwise (indicating imbalance). You may need to sit, stand, or lie down to comfortably reach over certain chakras. If you identify any imbalances, develop a self-care plan to help realign that chakra.

Blake Octavian Blair

 February 19
Tuesday

2nd ♌

☽ v/c 8:51 am

☽ → ♍ 9:47 am

Full Moon 10:54 am

Color of the Day: White
Incense of the Day: Basil

Sticks and Stones

Sticks and stones may break my bones, but words can also hurt me. Words have the power of an invisible dart that can wound your heart and soul. This spell is a balm for your wounded feelings.

On a brown piece of paper that has torn edges all on sides, write down the hurtful words. Turn the paper ninety degrees and write your full name across the words nine times. In an unending circle, without lifting your pen, write:

Your words have no power over me.

When you have finished writing the words, add a pinch of eucalyptus herb or essential oil to the center of the paper. Fold the paper away from you and tie it with a thread that has been knotted nine times. Burn the paper in a heatproof container. Flush the ashes down the toilet or throw them away somewhere far from your house.

Najah Lightfoot

 February 20
Wednesday

3rd ♍

☽ v/c 8:52 pm

Color of the Day: Yellow
Incense of the Day: Lavender

Transformation Spell

Wednesday is governed by the planet Mercury and the gods Mercury, Hermes, and Woden, who influence communication, understanding, divination, change, luck, good fortune, and gratitude, among other things. Use this transformation spell to inventory, understand, and communicate your blessings, simultaneously increasing your level of luck, good fortune, and gratitude.

Say:

Mercury, guide me that I may understand my blessings.

Then make a gratitude list. Say things such as:

I'm thankful for _____ .
I'm grateful for _____ .
I'm blessed that _____ .
Lucky, lucky me that _____ .
I'm divinely connected to _____ .
I'm so fortunate for _____ .
Thank you, thank you, thank you.

List the people, places, things, qualities, and experiences that enrich you. Notice that as you itemize your blessings, your perspective and your energy shift. Awareness and the practice of gratitude will magnetize you, attracting more good. Let Mercury help you communicate gratitude to others. Share your transformed energy and perspective, and inspire the same in others.

Repeat this technique regularly whenever you need to transform yourself.

Dallas Jennifer Cobb

February 21
Thursday

3rd ♍

☽ → ♎ 9:17 am

Color of the Day: Crimson
Incense of the Day: Clove

What Makes You happy?

Stop all your busyness for a few minutes and think about what makes you happy. Finding your favorite chocolate chip cookies on sale? Getting your device to work without making you crazy? Having a civilized conversation with an annoying person in which you began to "tame" them like the Fox tamed the Little Prince? Gazing at your laundry basket filled with clean, folded clothes and realizing you'll have clean clothes for a week or longer?

This may be the simplest spell you'll ever do. Visualize a circle with yourself and what makes you happy in the center. Open your arms as for a big hug. Visualize giving that hug to what makes you happy, whether it's concrete or abstract. Say out loud and with great enthusiasm:

Thank you, Goddess!
Thank you, thank you, thank you!

Barbara Ardinger

February 22
Friday

3rd ♎

Color of the Day: Pink
Incense of the Day: Thyme

Early Spring Cleaning – Renewal

We are between Imbolc and Ostara. Make this a weekend of change. Light candles, play music, and pour a beverage. Write a list. Sort through all the holiday items and donate anything no longer wanted. Get out all the clothing for the next season, and clean, repair, or toss it. Then repack the freshened clothing. Maybe it's time to let go of some of your book collection. Do you need new dishes, glasses, or cutlery? Empty kitchen cabinets and toss outdated food, clean the shelves, and put down new shelf paper. Do not allow yourself to be overwhelmed. Choose one to three chores, and follow through the entire weekend. Put on a slow cooker meal on Saturday morning, something that will last through Sunday afternoon. When all is done on Sunday, be sure to thank the gods and goddesses of the hearth and home, especially Hera, for all of their help:

Clutter begone, set a moderate pace,
Clean and clear, now creating space,
For the good, this little spell.
My home is blessed and all is well.

Emyme

February 23
Saturday

3rd ♎
☽ v/c 10:11 am
☽ → ♏ 10:56 am

Color of the Day: Gray
Incense of the Day: Patchouli

Sadie Hawkins' Guide to Tantra

Every second, like right now and next week, some girl, boy, or hijra somewhere is discovering the pleasure palace that is their own natural body. As Pagans we unabashedly and playfully celebrate the natural empowerment of our sexuality. Self-pleasure is a healthy, liberating, and joyful experience when you worship nature. Taking yourself to natural stages of wonder and delight can be spiritually as well as physically pleasurable. Body exploration and arousal are innocent ways to discover the creative magic of sex.

So go on, dear reader: take a few minutes and love yourself today. Find one pleasurable and naturally attractive part of yourself and fixate your attention on it to gratifying singularity. Immaculately conceive of a world where original sin is replaced with human anatomy and sexuality facts, leaving no room for shame in that educated and sexy mind of yours!

Estha McNevin

February 24
Sunday

3rd ♏

Color of the Day: Gold
Incense of the Day: Almond

Manifest happiness at Work Spell

Work is a necessity for many of us, but sometimes we work in an environment that can make the necessary unenjoyable. Cast this spell to bring happiness to your workplace and help lighten up the environment when in need.

Take a swatch of yellow fabric about the size of your open hand and into it place the following:

- 3 pinches chamomile herb
- 2 pinches hyssop
- 1 pinch frankincense
- 3 pinches eyebright
- A small piece of paper that has the astrological symbol for the sun (☉) drawn on it

Fold the edges of the fabric inward, creating a charm bag. Use gold thread to seal the bag, and chant:

With the sun I light the way,
bringing about joy and play.

With these herbs I unlock the sun,
releasing camaraderie and fun!

Keep this charm with you at work and recite the chant at the start of each work day.

Devin hunter

February 25
Monday

3rd ♏

☽ v/c 7:14 am

☽ → ♐ 4:19 pm

Color of the Day: White
Incense of the Day: Rosemary

A Wishing Tree Spell

With spring not far away, this is a good time to create your own wishing tree. To do this, first write a wish on a strip of fabric, using a pen or marker. To charge your wish, tuck it beneath your pillow for one night. Don't be surprised if you receive a prophetic dream. The next day, find a tree or shrub in bud that appeals to you. Tie your wish on one of its branches. This will be your wishing tree. As its buds begin to swell, your wish will start working in the unseen realm. After your wish comes true, remove your wish from the tree and bury it near the tree as an offering to your wishing tree. This tree or shrub and you are now connected. Use it again for your wishes and magic.

James Kambos

 **February 26**
Tuesday

3rd ♐

4th Quarter 6:28 am

Color of the Day: Maroon
Incense of the Day: Cinnamon

Maple Syrup Love Spells

The sweetness of maple syrup, and its association with warmth and growth, make it perfect for love spells. Maple syrup is basically the "blood" of the maple tree. The sun warms the tree in late winter and sap starts to flow through the tree's veins. The sap is collected for making maple syrup, sugar, and candy. Charge a bottle of local maple syrup with love, and use it in the following ways:

- Add a small dab of syrup to your bathwater, along with some rose petals or lavender, for a refreshing, romance-attracting bath.

- Make some maple cookies in the shape of hearts and serve them to your loved ones.

- Pour some syrup in a pretty jar and add lavender and rose petals to it. Let it sit for a week, then give it as a gift. When the recipient eats it, they will ingest loving energy.

- Use maple syrup as a sugar replacement in hot beverages. Have some love with your morning coffee!

- Carefully dribble the syrup into the snow in the shape of a symbol or sigil that represents love, such as a heart or an X. Let the snow melt and carry your sweet wishes into the earth.

Kate Freuler

 February 27
Wednesday

4th ♐

Color of the Day: Brown
Incense of the Day: Honeysuckle

Ritual honoring Air

This ritual celebrates the air element and helps you incorporate its characteristics into your life. Air represents the mind, intellect, creativity, beginnings, and communication. Choose one (or more) of these aspects on which to focus, or include all of them in your visualization.

Select an object to represent air, and place it on your altar. It can be a feather, for example, or a photo or drawing of the sky. Flutes and other wind instruments are also symbolic of air. Speak these words:

I honor the element of air—
the wind, the movement of life,
and the changes it brings;
I move with ease in the breeze,
ride the air like untethered leaves,
without fear or worry
where it may lead, accepting
adventure and discovery.

Ember Grant

February 28
Thursday

4th ♐

☽ v/c 1:17 am

☽ → ♑ 1:48 am

Color of the Day: White
Incense of the Day: Carnation

Winter Slower Energy Meditation

The energy of the earth slows during the winter months, even in the places where it stays relatively warm, although it might be less obvious there. Our ancestors slowed down with the season, as the days grew shorter and there were no crops to tend. They had no electric lights or television, so they went to bed early or told stories by the fire. These days it is harder to slow down, so use this simple meditation to help you remember to go with the naturally slower flow of the winter. Start by lighting a white candle and taking deep, slow breaths as you say this to yourself, either silently or aloud:

It is winter, and the world is quiet.

I will be quiet too

*And slow my pace to match
that of the earth.*

Quiet and slow, slow and quiet,

Breathing in, breathing out,

Slowly.

Deborah Blake

March

M arch is upon us! March is a month of unpredictable weather. Will the weather spirits decide to bring us a last hurrah of winter in the form of a blustery snowstorm or instead bring us signs of spring's beginning in the form of budding trees and perhaps rain showers sprinkled with mild, sunny days? There really is no telling! However, for those of us who follow the Wheel of the Year, the spring equinox is a time of new beginnings, regardless of the weather.

Rituals of spring and new beginnings will take place around the globe this month. Druids still gather at Stonehenge to welcome the rising sun on the morning of the equinox. March also is the time to celebrate the festival of Holi, popular in India and Nepal. People engage in paint fights, covering each other in festive splatters of vibrant color, welcoming the arrival of spring and all its vibrancy.

In March, however you choose to celebrate, work the magick of new beginnings!

Blake Octavian Blair

March 1
Friday

4th ♑

Color of the Day: Coral
Incense of the Day: Violet

Doing Magic in Public

Sometimes we need to do some small magic in public where people can see us. But we obviously cannot set up an altar while we're sitting in a meeting at work. What to do? First, visualize. Second, use your forefinger as your wand. Start with small magic. You can do bigger work at home or with your circle or coven.

Visualize what you want to happen. Imagine that it can "hear" you. Using your projective hand (right, if you're right-handed), draw little deosil (clockwise) circles with your forefinger to get your target's attention.

When you've got its attention, use your receptive forefinger and draw deosil circles to stir up some action, like maybe to pull some money or other treasure in your direction. When you feel it coming, grab it with your forefinger and thumb. If you're working in public, you'll merely look like a very twitchy person. (Please note that this will not work with cats.)

Barbara Ardinger

March 2
Saturday

4th ♑

☽ v/c 1:47 pm
☽ → ♒ 2:06 pm

Color of the Day: Indigo
Incense of the Day: Ivy

There and Back Again, Bilbo

Are you longing to travel like Bilbo Baggins, there and back again? Then take a minute today to begin a journal in anticipation of your voyage. While adding ideas to your diary, focus your creative manifesting powers imaginatively. Collecting postcards and travel magazines will help you fill your mind with possibilities, hotel locations, or document details such as train times and bus schedules.

Fully calculate the cost of your adventure and find a way to achieve your travel goal with micro-saving methods. Working hard to research and discover another city or country before you travel is essential. A simple travel log can become an ironic memento of home and abroad, because the more we journal our adventures, the more we long for home. The road will rise to meet your magick, dear reader, especially if you've a pinch of intentional planning and the good luck charm of a journal and a pen in your right side pocket.

Estha McNevin

March 3
Sunday

4th ≈

Color of the Day: Yellow
Incense of the Day: Marigold

Caregiver Appreciation Day

Many people look after those who are sick, disabled, or elderly. Maybe you or your loved ones have benefited from them, or will in the future. Today is Caregiver Appreciation Day, a good time to honor them and their hard work.

This is an altar spell, so you'll need your altar, a small green candle in a safe glass, and a source of fire. You also need an image of your favorite healing deity. Cast a circle, light the candle, and invoke your patron of healing. State your intent to honor caregivers. Focus on the candle and recall occasions when someone has looked after you or those you love. Send some energy into the light. Ask your healing patron to direct the energy to the caregivers who need it most. Thank them for their contributions.

After you finish, release the deity and the circle. Allow the candle to burn out safely.

Elizabeth Barrette

March 4
Monday

4th ≈

Color of the Day: Gray
Incense of the Day: Lily

Appreciation at Work Spell

Pisces rules over us now and is reminding us that it is important to feel appreciated and respected, especially where we spend most of our time. Cast this spell to bring about a subtle awareness to your employer and coworkers about how valuable you are to the team. Grab the business card of your superior and write your name over their contact information three times, then anoint it lightly with lavender oil. Hold the business card with both hands and enchant it by saying:

> *See me for what I am,*
> *someone deserving more.*
>
> *See me for what I am,*
> *an eagle who can soar.*
>
> *Appreciate me for what I do,*
> *I need to know you care.*
>
> *Appreciate me for what I do,*
> *open your heart and share.*

Put the card in your shoe and leave it there until you feel appreciated.

Devin Hunter

March 5
Tuesday

4th ♒

☽ v/c 3:05 am

☽ → ♓ 3:11 am

Color of the Day: Black
Incense of the Day: Cedar

Mardi Gras (Fat Tuesday)

A Feast Before Fasting

The end of Mardi Gras is upon us, today being Fat Tuesday. Adorn yourself with the colors of the season: emerald green, golden yellow, and royal purple. Partake in pancakes, fried breads, or pastries. All of these foods stem from the tradition of using up all the lard and grains stored for the winter in preparation for the fasting of Lent. Pre-Christian, this fasting coincided with the winter food stores being almost depleted. These modern times allow us to pick and choose the extent of our hunger level. However, to be true to the sentiment, as you prepare for indulgence, take some time today to rid your pantry of some over-comforting foods. Replace with fresh vegetables and fruits particular to your part of the world. Plan some light meals for Ash Wednesday.

After that, raise your glass and start celebrating!

Look at this abundance of riches, prepared for celebration.

Tomorrow begins the fasting, tonight is for the feasting.

Join in, join hands, strike up the flames, strike up the music.

Fall into the revelry, huzzah!

Emyme

March 6
Wednesday

4th ♓

New Moon 11:04 am

Color of the Day: White
Incense of the Day: Marjoram

Ash Wednesday

Forgive Yourself Spell

Today we have a new moon occurring while the sun is in emotional Pisces. This is a perfect day to unburden yourself of any feelings of guilt. Use this new moon to forgive yourself for any mistakes you've made and start fresh.

For this ritual you'll need a sheet of plain white paper, a blue ink pen, a few twigs, some dried sage, and a feather. You'll also need a cauldron or a heatproof dish. On the paper write any mistakes you've made and feel sorry for. Break the twigs into the cauldron and ignite them. Crumple the paper and place it on the flames. Now sprinkle the sage over the flames. Fan the smoke over you using the feather. Let the smoke carry away any feelings of guilt. When the ashes are cold, sprinkle them in a garden or compost pile. Forgive yourself and move forward.

James Kambos

March 7
Thursday

1st ♈ ♓

☽ v/c 2:08 pm

☽ → ♈ 3:27 pm

Color of the Day: Turquoise
Incense of the Day: Balsam

Self-Sufficiency Spell

Thursday is ruled by Jupiter, known astrologically as the Greater Benefic. Jupiter is expansive, bringing opportunities, increase, generosity, good fortune, and luck. Since today is a day for abundance, protection, prosperity, strength, wealth, and healing, let's use this "great benefic" energy for a self-sufficiency spell. If we are self-sufficient (financially, emotionally, socially, and even sexually), it frees us to make very different choices, ones not based on need.

You'll need a photo of yourself, some money, a wrapped candy or chocolate bar, and a blue cloth or ribbon. Place the photo on your altar, standing up, looking out. Say:

Jupiter, expand my horizons,
help me govern my life.

Place the money in front of the photo. Say:

I have wealth and resources.

Place the candy. Say:

I have sweet sustainability.

Surround these with the blue cloth or ribbon. Say:

Jupiter's energy encircles me,

Expanding self-sufficiency.

The Greater Benefic blesses me.

So mote it be.

Repeat as needed.

Dallas Jennifer Cobb

March 8
Friday

1st ♈

Color of the Day: Purple
Incense of the Day: Cypress

Candle Spell for Women

Today is International Women's Day. To strengthen your relationships with the women in your life and to focus on awareness of women's issues, begin by carving the symbol for "woman" (♀) into a purple or white votive candle. Place appropriate symbols on your altar, such as goddess statues, pictures of women you wish to honor, etc.

As the candle burns, consider all the ways you can acknowledge the women in your life. Research issues of concern today, and take some action or make a donation. You can also show appreciation for the women in your life with a kind gesture or gift.

In addition, if you're a woman, do something special for yourself today.

As you light the candle, chant:

To those who suffer, bring relief,
alleviate their pain and grief.

Satisfy all those in need,
honor them by word and deed.

Allow the candle to burn out safely.

Ember Grant

March 9
Saturday

1st ♈

☽ v/c 12:14 pm

Color of the Day: Blue
Incense of the Day: Pine

Saturnal Protection Bag

Saturday's energies are aligned with Saturn, which makes it a great day for some protection magick. Gather the following items, all of which align with the planet Saturn and have protective energies:

• A small square of black cloth or felt about four inches square
• 1 tablespoon dried thyme
• A small piece of jet stone
• A piece of twine or ribbon

Lay the cloth flat on your workspace, and place the thyme in a pile on the cloth. Add the jet stone on top of the pile, and place your hands over the arrangement, palms downward. Envision your hands charging the items, and visualize them beginning to glow, emanating protective energies. Draw up the corners of the cloth and tie with the twine, holding protective intentions. Then blow three times onto the bag. Carry the bag when you feel you need an extra protective boost from unfriendly energies.

Blake Octavian Blair

March 10
Sunday

1st ♈

☽ → ♉ 3:10 am

Color of the Day: Orange
Incense of the Day: Hyacinth

Daylight Saving Time
begins at 2:00 a.m.

The Wibby-Wobbly Timey-Wimey Spell

Have you ever wanted to travel through time? Aside from going back and witnessing the building of the pyramids or killing Hitler, what if we could get back a bit of the time we have spent, so we can spend it again?

For this spell you will need a non-digital clock (one with hands).

Set the clock so that it reads one hour ahead of the current time. So if it is 4:00 p.m., set it for 5:00 p.m.

Ground and center. Focus on the clock the same way you might a crystal ball or scrying mirror. Enter into a trance. Say:

It is [time on clock]. (x3)

Tick, tock, tick, tock,

So go the workings of my magic clock.

Tock, tack, tock, tack,

*Slow do we turn now the
hands of time back.*

Forcibly turn the clock hands back an hour so that it now reads correctly, "giving" you that hour. Spend it wisely.

Storm Faerywolf

March 11
Monday

1st ♉

Color of the Day: Silver
Incense of the Day: Hyssop

Nurturing Relationships with Fun

By the end of winter, it isn't unusual to find yourself growing restless and impatient for spring and cranky with those around you. This can be especially true in colder climates where you might be stuck inside with people. Take this restless and impatient energy and turn it into something fun instead. Have a family game night, challenge your colleagues to a good-natured competition, or invite your friends over for a silly movie. Say this spell to help channel that restless energy into more productive paths that nurture rather than strain your relationships:

As winter winds to an end and I find myself restless and rude,

Help me to find a path to improve my mind and my mood.

Help relationships to shine as we wait for the summer sun,

Turning winter's dark and gloom into playfulness and silly fun.

Deborah Blake

March 12
Tuesday

1st ♉

☽ v/c 5:31 am
☽ → ♊ 11:48 am

Color of the Day: Red
Incense of the Day: Ginger

Comical Reflection

On this date in 1951, the comic strip *Dennis the Menace* made its newspaper debut. Comic strips are an enduring part of our culture, both in print and in the present-day online editions. Comic strips provide not only a laugh but also humorous and sometimes stark commentary on topics ranging from growing up to office dynamics and politics.

Today, look in print or online at a few comic strips. Find one with a message that truly resonates with you. Cut or print it out, and hang or keep it near your workspace today. Reflect on why it resonates with you. Does it mirror something neutral, positive, or negative in your life? On paper, jot down actions you can take to make the situation you're contemplating better, or to maintain it if it's already good, or how to just be more in the moment when the situation arises. Hang the paper in your sacred space and review as necessary.

Blake Octavian Blair

March 13
Wednesday

1st ♊

Color of the Day: Brown
Incense of the Day: Lavender

March hare Spell

We've all heard the old idiom "mad as a March hare." The saying stems from the bizarre behavior that European hares display during mating season. In their quest for romance, the hare becomes a true party animal, with bursting energy, social antics, and even feats of strength. The playful spirit of the March hare can get your spring off to an energetic start and attract some like-minded people to share the fun and lusty vibes of the season.

For this spell you will need a rabbit's foot key chain (synthetic is fine!), a picture of a March hare, and some early spring flowers.

Lay the faux rabbit's foot on top of the picture, and make a circle around it with the flowers. Imagine the bursting, happy energy of the flowers infusing the charm. See the frolicking, energetic social vitality of the March hare filling the rabbit's foot.

Carry this charm and let it bring some fresh, fun influences, friends, and romance into your sphere.

Kate Freuler

March 14
Thursday

1st ♊
2nd Quarter 6:27 am
☽ v/c 8:30 am
☽ → ♋ 5:49 pm

Color of the Day: Green
Incense of the Day: Jasmine

My One-in-7.5 Billion for as Long as It Takes Love Spell

Love-doves and mating animals of every persuasion observe the euphoria of this special time of affection, mating, and natural bliss. If you are seeking your one true love, try this simple spell using organic birdseed to cast your path to a conjugal destiny. Procure seven pounds of local bird feed and weave a love spell today, laying a trail of seeds right back to you.

Unabashedly sprinkle birdseed everywhere you go. Draw in avian tenderness while feeding the birds of spring gently. Within your longing, recite the Latin prayer below each time you toss seeds; attach a desired quality to each handful you sprinkle in the name of love.

Seal this spell with a steadfast kiss and the birds of spring will forever bless you:

> O' turturem columbae, columbam,
> parus caeruleus, et avem;
>
> Venus, mei ad me, verus
> amor meam producat.
>
> (O turtle dove, pigeon, and chickadee;
>
> Venus, bring my true love unto me.)
>
> Estha McNevin

March 15
Friday

2nd ♋

Color of the Day: Rose
Incense of the Day: Orchid

Spell to Reveal hidden Enemies

If you suspect there may be some foes hiding among your friends, try this spell to compel the individual to reveal their true colors. For each person you suspect may not have your best interests at heart, write their whole name on the shell of an uncooked egg with a black permanent marker. Place the eggs in a pot and cover them with cold water. Bring the water to a boil as you chant:

> No one here can hide their truth, bad eggs will crack, for sure, forsooth.

After the water has been boiling for about a minute, turn off the heat and cover the pot. Wait fifteen minutes. If any of the eggs are cracked, keep a close eye on the person whose name it bears, as hidden aspects of their intentions and actions will soon come to light.

Melanie Marquis

March 16
Saturday

2nd ♋

☽ v/c 2:03 pm

☽ → ♌ 8:57 pm

Color of the Day: Blue
Incense of the Day: Sandalwood

healing Regret, Shame, and Remorse

Nathaniel Hawthorne's masterwork, *The Scarlet Letter*, was published on this day in 1850. Shame, regret, and remorse are tough emotions. They can take a toll on one's spirit and place a burden upon the heart. Many times it is easier to forgive others than it is to forgive ourselves.

We all make mistakes. The lesson is to learn from those mistakes and move on with your life. It's been said that the universe keeps bringing lessons around in stronger and stronger ways until you finally get it. Don't let the universe use a sledgehammer to bring you into awareness! Admit your mistake and move forward. Allow for the expansiveness of soul that comes with humility.

Tonight, add three drops of rose essential oil to a spray bottle filled with distilled water. Spray your room with the rose water. Wish yourself pleasant dreams. Awake tomorrow to a new day and new beginning.

Najah Lightfoot

 March 17
Sunday

2nd ♌

Color of the Day: Amber
Incense of the Day: Frankincense

Saint Patrick's Day

A Prosperity Spell

Long before there was a Saint Patrick's Day, some ancient peoples used this day to perform rituals for prosperity, abundance, and fertility. Here is a spell appropriate for today. You'll need a green or gold candle and an ivy plant. Light the candle and water the ivy. Gaze at the flame and say:

Prosperity, abundance, and fertility,

You are welcome in my home.

So mote it be.

Then snuff out the candle safely. Tend the ivy plant and give it a special place in your home. As it flourishes, your spell will begin working. Occasionally remove a few leaves from the ivy and scatter them outside your front door. As you do so, think of or say the charm again.

James Kambos

March 18
Monday

2nd ♌

☽ v/c 11:19 am

☽ → ♍ 9:41 pm

Color of the Day: Ivory
Incense of the Day: Clary sage

Protection During a Storm

Spring often brings tumultuous storms we cannot avoid. During these storms, visualize the elemental effects being diminished and see the storm passing without doing damage. Hold a piece of pyrite, if you have one, and visualize it as a shield. If you don't have pyrite, use a clear quartz crystal. Recite this chant as many times as you wish:

> Blowing wind, do no harm.
>
> What you touch may bend, not break.
>
> Driving rain, do no harm.
>
> No flooding here; thirst will slake.
>
> Lightning bolt, do no harm.
>
> No home or life your fire will take.
>
> Pounding hail, do no harm.
>
> Your falling here no mess will make.
>
> Storm will safely pass us by,
>
> Giving way to peaceful sky.

Ember Grant

March 19
Tuesday

2nd ♍

Color of the Day: Gray
Incense of the Day: Geranium

Ask Father Mars for help

March is, of course, ruled by Mars. So is Tuesday (*mardi* in French). Originally called Marspiter (Father Mars), Mars was an Etruscan and Sabine agricultural god. His mother was Juno, his father, a flower. After Mars fathered Romulus and Remus and moved to the city, the Romans built him a temple on the Palatine Hill, and he became a god of defensive warfare because the Romans needed someone to defend their fields and produce.

If you're feeling unsafe where you live or work, call on Mars for protection:

> Great Father Mars, please
> come to my aid.
>
> [Explain the danger you're in.]
>
> Father Mars, you protect your
> people and your territory.
>
> I am your friend. Please
> send protection to me.

When I needed protection from violent neighbors, I appealed to Mars. He sent two legionaries to stand at my door. No one else could see them, but they kept me safe.

Barbara Ardinger

March 20
Wednesday

2nd ♍

☽ v/c 11:22 am

☉ → ♈ 5:58 pm

☽ → ♎ 9:28 pm

Full Moon 9:43 pm

Color of the Day: Yellow
Incense of the Day: Bay laurel

Spring Equinox – Ostara

Persephone Oil

Today is a powerful day indeed: the moon is full and it is the vernal equinox! Persephone rises from the underworld full of potential and warmth, ushering in the brilliance of lunar manifestation. Today is a great day for mixing and empowering Persephone Oil for work that will bring truth where there are secrets, light where there is darkness, and hope where there is fear.

Combine one part each cypress, ylang-ylang, and dragon's blood oil, then dilute by half with a carrier oil (such as sweet almond, fractionated coconut, or olive oil). Place the mixture someplace where you can empower it under the moonlight tonight, and say:

Persephone, Persephone,
bring me your rays.

Persephone, Persephone,
bring warmer days!

Allow your Persephone Oil to soak up lunar energy tonight, then store it away from direct light afterward.

Devin Hunter

March 21
Thursday

3rd ♎

Color of the Day: White
Incense of the Day: Clove

Purim (begins at
sundown on March 20)

Purim Protection Spell

Today is Purim, a Jewish holiday that celebrates the salvation of the Jews from Haman's plot to kill them all. You don't have to be Jewish to observe this holiday as a reprieve from intolerance and genocide. It's a great day for casting protection spells.

You'll need a symbol for any god or goddess of protection, along with a vessel to carry the spell. Money works, and so do hamantaschen or other edibles. Cast a circle, then invoke your favorite protective deity and ask for their help. Focus on your desire to give protection, then put that into the vessel. Give thanks to your protective patron, then release them and your circle.

Distribute the vessel to people who need protection or other resources. Ideally they should be folks you know personally, but if you don't know anyone suitable, you may give to a charity instead.

Elizabeth Barrette

March 22
Friday

3rd ♎

☽ v/c 2:10 pm

☽ → ♏ 10:16 pm

Color of the Day: Coral
Incense of the Day: Mint

Worry Bubble

Humans may be hard-wired to worry. Our awareness of danger has allowed us to survive and evolve. But there is a difference between normal concern and preparedness and the crazy-making worry about things we cannot control. Additionally, if our thoughts become things (as many believe), then it follows that scary thoughts may bring about the feared calamity.

If you find yourself tipping into that crazy-worry state of mind, bring yourself up short and deliberately change the scenario. Envision a large, clear bubble of protection around the person, place, or thing that causes concern and say:

> My (family, home, car, workplace) is protected.

Simply say or think the basic *All is well, all will be well, all will always be well*, and you have done all you can to dispel the negative and get back on track.

Say:

Safe, secure, and solvent,

Happy, healthy, and whole,

My family is protected.

All is well, life is good.

Emyme

March 23
Saturday

3rd ♏

Color of the Day: Indigo
Incense of the Day: Magnolia

The Keys of Life

Gift a couple the keys to happiness and success with this fun spell. Gather seven old skeleton keys and a golden key ring. Attach a rainbow ribbon and a shipping tag to each key. Upon each tag write the Venusian keys to love:

1: **Trust**, exhibited as equally reciprocated

2: **Understanding**, extended to others always

3: **Love**, given as well as received freely

4: **Forgiveness**, grappled with regularly

5: **Gratitude**, exhibited daily

6: **Resources**, united and equally occupied

7: **Vision**, shared goals for the future secured

Tie all of the ribbons in multiple bows and place them all on the golden ring. Place one final tag on the ring and write:

In thought, speech, and action, I pledge.

Gift this charm to couples as a blessing evocative of the golden rules of cooperative happiness in partnership. Consult elders in your family to learn new keys and create a tradition of passing on the wisdom that works.

Estha McNevin

March 24
Sunday

3rd ♏

☽ v/c 10:24 pm

Color of the Day: Orange
Incense of the Day: Heliotrope

Aquamarine Ritual

Aquamarine is the birthstone for March. Today, utilize its strong protective magick to ensure your inner tranquility.

Go to a gem or bead shop and purchase four pieces of aquamarine.

Grab a small shovel and head out to your favorite place for ritual work, on your property or elsewhere. A beach or the forest works well.

With each step you take, say:

Vitality, health, hope, tranquility.

This will set your mind at ease and plant you firmly in the here and now.

Once you reach your location, face north, bury a piece of aquamarine, and say firmly:

Vitality.

Face east, bury the second piece of aquamarine, and recite:

Health.

Facing south, bury the third piece of stone and say:

Hope.

Face west, bury the final piece of gemstone, and affirm:

Tranquility.

Sit in the center of this power circle. Close your eyes and soak in the qualities you have planted.

Leave the aquamarines buried for a fortnight. Return and dig up the stones. Now you have four charged aquamarine stones ready to use in other sacred work.

Stephanie Rose Bird

March 25
Monday

3rd ♏

☽ → ♐ 2:06 am

Color of the Day: White
Incense of the Day: Neroli

Remembering the Ancestors of Place

On this day in 1634, the first colonists arrived in what is now southern Maryland. They were Catholics seeking to escape religious persecution. Let us all take some time today to do some research on those who occupied our lands before us: the Ancestors of Place. We may not think or be much like them. However, we are indeed connected through our physical occupation of the same lands. Whether we are proud of our ancestors or vehemently disagree with them, there are lessons to be learned from them.

Light a white candle upon your altar and anoint it with a magical oil or holy water of your choice. Allow the Ancestors of the Land to offer you their lessons so you can glean wisdom from their lives. Then allow the candle to burn down safely as you research those who came before you.

Blake Octavian Blair

March 26
Tuesday

3rd ♐

☽ v/c 10:37 pm

Color of the Day: Scarlet
Incense of the Day: Ylang-ylang

Spring Seed Blessing

In most places in the country, it is too early to actually put seeds in the ground. But just as we plan ahead and prepare for the growing times ahead, we can do magical work to prepare ourselves to be fertile ground for prosperity and abundance in our own lives. Even if you don't garden, you can use seeds as the symbol for the potential that lies in the seasons ahead. Seeds are all about potential, holding an entire future plant inside.

To do this spell, use a green candle, a packet of seeds, and, if you want, a list of things you wish to have grow in abundance in your life. Light the candle, read your list, and visualize what you want. Hold the seeds up to the sun and say:

Bless these seeds, a symbol of abundance and potential,

That my life will grow and blossom in the months to come.

Deborah Blake

March 27
Wednesday

3rd ♐

☽ → ♑ 10:07 am

Color of the Day: Topaz
Incense of the Day: Honeysuckle

Interdependence Incantation

An incantation is the use of words as a magic spell, a chant that produces magical results.

Carl Jung believed that everyone has internalized energy: men have an inner feminine called the *anima*, and women have an inner masculine called the *animus*. To be happy, healthy, and whole, we need to develop the strengths of both the masculine and the feminine.

With the right hand symbolizing the masculine and the left hand symbolizing the feminine, clasp your hands together to symbolize their interdependence. Envision your masculine and feminine energies intertwined and interdependent, like the two parts of the yin-yang. Incant:

Like yin and yang, black and white,

Are male and female, day and night.

Sun and moon, earth and sea,

Two parts intertwine in me.

Gentle and forceful, slow and fast,

Emotion and mind, future and past.

Balanced and powerful,
stable and strong,

Intertwined in the present
is where I belong.

Dallas Jennifer Cobb

March 28
Thursday

3rd ♑

4th Quarter 12:10 am

Color of the Day: Purple
Incense of the Day: Carnation

Egg Purification Spell

During a time when there are disagreements, upset feelings, or stress in the home, it may be necessary to cleanse a room or area in order to move forward with forgiveness.

Eggs are symbols of fertility, hope, and renewal almost all over the world, and are also believed to cleanse and heal situations and people. Draw an X with black marker onto an egg while visualizing the situation or person you'd like to remove negativity from. Light a white candle. Carefully pass the egg over the flame without touching it, and imagine the egg is surrounded by an orb of purifying white light. This light has the power to absorb and immobilize negativity.

Hide the egg somewhere in the house for three days. Allow it to drain all unwanted resentment or fear from the home. Afterward, thank it and break it into the garbage or compost to dispose of it.

Kate Freuler

 ## March 29
Friday

4th ♑

☽ v/c 8:05 pm

☽ → ♒ 9:46 pm

Color of the Day: Pink
Incense of the Day: Thyme

The Stone of Healing

This is a simple charm to give an extra boost to the healing process. (It is not to be used in place of proper medical care.) You will need a piece of sugilite or mangano calcite. Both of these stones are renowned for their healing properties, sugilite helping to access the higher vibrational pattern of perfect health to be channeled into the physical, and mangano calcite enhancing one's natural healing energies.

Hold the stone in your projective (dominant) hand. Focus on the person who has the ailment, imagining them as being completely healthy and strong. Say the following three times:

Full of vigor,

Strength of stone,

Fount of wellness,

It is done.

Take three breaths and blow out onto the stone, focusing on the person as being healed and full of life force. Give the stone to them as a healing charm.

Storm Faerywolf

March 30
Saturday

4th ≈

Color of the Day: Brown
Incense of the Day: Rue

Spell for Balance

For this spell you'll need one blank sheet of paper and two circles of colored paper. Divide one of the circles into pie slices to represent the things in your life you're currently pouring your energy into: family, friends, work, play, hobbies, self, hopes and dreams. Make the slices proportionally sized to reflect the amount of energy you are giving to each aspect of your life. Glue this circle onto the blank sheet of paper. What do you see? Now divide the other circle into pie slices to represent how you would prefer to spend your energies in an ideal world. Divide your "ideal" pie however you like, then glue it on top of the original circle to cover it. Hang this somewhere in your home as a magickal charm and daily reminder to strive for the balance your heart desires.

Melanie Marquis

March 31
Sunday

4th ≈

☽ v/c 11:02 pm

Color of the Day: Gold
Incense of the Day: Eucalyptus

Turn Back the Hands of Time

On this day in 1918, Daylight Saving Time went into effect for the very first time. When the first people to experience Daylight Saving Time turned their clocks backward, they all became magicians, controlling time and using it to manipulate the daylight hours for personal gain. (And people say they don't believe in magick!)

Take a moment to think about how time affects your life. When does time move fast? When does it move slowly? When do you have too much time and not enough?

Sit down and draw a large clock on a piece of paper. Underneath the clock, write:

Time is an illusion. All that changes is my perception of it.

Place your paper clock in a closet and close the door. Once a week open the door, look at your clock, and see if your perception of time has changed.

Najah Lightfoot

April

This month we move from dark to light, from cold to warm, from brown to green. April is a magical month that starts with April Fools' Day and ends on the eve of May Day, begins with a joke and ends with an outdoor sleep-out. Here in Ontario, Canada, the average temperature at the beginning of April is close to freezing. It's common to have snow on the ground. Throughout April a magical transformation occurs: the temperature climbs as high as 66 degrees Fahrenheit (19 degrees Celsius) and flowers bloom.

Post-equinox, the days grow longer. Between April 1 and 30, the daylight increases from 12 hours and 46 minutes to 14 hours and 8 minutes. As the sun travels northward, it climbs in the sky. Not only do days lengthen, but shadows shorten as well. It is inviting to get outdoors. Like the plants that need sunlight to conduct photosynthesis, we humans need sunlight to help manufacture vitamin D.

This month, make time to enjoy the outdoors. Get out in the daylight, take evening walks in the twilight after dinner, contemplate your garden, and turn your face toward the sun at every chance. With winter coming to an end, now is your time to transform.

Dallas Jennifer Cobb

April 1
Monday

4th ≈

☽ → ♓ 10:48 am

Color of the Day: White
Incense of the Day: Lily

April Fools' Day – All Fools' Day

A Fool in Every Nook and Cranny

Select the Fool card (trump zero) from your favorite Tarot deck and make ninety-three photocopies of the card. As you go about your day, distribute your Holy Fools across the world. Place them in fun, creative, silly, or meaningful places. Graffiti each one with cloud speech bubbles, quotes, or sayings that feel wise, funny, and insightful.

Each person who sees the cards will be amused or affected by your willfully foolish magic today if you pick your locations with careful delight. Write love and thank-you notes; pepper your path with the Punch, to remind you that only a fool thinks they know everything. How long will fools stick around? Search for the meaning behind that last Fool standing or any Fools that may find their way back to you somehow. Using the Fool to discover the synchronistic wonders of magick will help you to learn more about your own highest esoteric potential, all jokes aside!

Estha McNevin

 April 2
Tuesday

4th ♓

Color of the Day: Maroon
Incense of the Day: Bayberry

International Children's Book Day

Today is International Children's Book Day. This is a time to celebrate reading in general and children's books in particular. It also meshes well with many Pagan deities such as Seshat, goddess of writing.

Observe this holiday by celebrating books and children. Focus especially on children who rarely get to hear their own stories, such as young Pagans and people from different ethnic groups. Most classic children's literature is very Christian and lacks diversity. So volunteer to do a reading, or donate some children's books with more diverse content. There are many beautiful books about myths from around the world, and a handful of explicitly Pagan ones if you know someplace where those would be welcome.

This holiday doesn't need a lot of fancy spellcasting. Keep the focus on the kids and the books. Just say a little prayer to Seshat or another writing patron when you do your thing.

Elizabeth Barrette

April 3
Wednesday

4th ♓

☽ v/c 11:36 am

☽ → ♈ 10:56 pm

Color of the Day: Yellow

Incense of the Day: Lilac

April Love

It's April and love is in the air. Here is an April love spell. You'll need two pink candles and a bouquet of pansies. Perform this spell over three nights. On the first night, place the candles at opposite sides of your altar or a table. Between them place the pansies. (The pansies should stay fresh for three days. If not, replace them.) Light the candles and say:

> Pansies, love magnet that you are,
>
> Bring me the perfect love.
>
> It may come from near or far,
>
> Just make it true and make it sweet.
>
> Let it be a love that makes
> my world complete.

Repeat this charm for two more nights, but each night move the candles closer until they're next to each other. On the last night, let the candles burn out safely, and hide them until the spell works. Then discard them if you wish.

James Kambos

April 4
Thursday

4th ♈

Color of the Day: Green

Incense of the Day: Balsam

Jupiterian Prosperity Booster

Thursday is the day of the week that is associated with the planet and the god Jupiter. Jupiter rules over prosperity and abundance. True abundance in life isn't measured in dollars, but in love, friendship, and having enough to eat and a happy home. Today, let's do a little magickal booster to manifest those things.

Gather images of the Ten of Pentacles and the Ten of Cups from the tarot. These cards together depict happy homes and families and security of resources. On top of the images place a bowl containing any combination of the herbs and spices nutmeg, cinnamon, cloves, and mint. Place a chalice of your favorite drink or clean water near the arrangement. Light a candle and recite:

> Abundance, as it is readily
> apparent here,
>
> May you bring more as you stay near.
>
> Health, wealth, and
> abundance be mine,
>
> As reflected in this image to
> the eyes of the divine.
>
> Blessed be.

Blake Octavian Blair

April 5
Friday

4th ♈

ℕew Moon 4:50 am

☾ v/c 10:15 pm

Color of the Day: Rose
Incense of the Day: Vanilla

Meditation for Renewal

On this new moon, make way for renewal in your life. Often we think we want change, but we're not really prepared for it. Tonight, open yourself to whatever new beginning or restart you may need. Light a black votive candle (or white as a substitute) and focus on something specific you need to renew. Do you have neglected projects or responsibilities? Something you're putting off? Or maybe you just feel worn down and need a boost of energy. Find a comfortable place to sit or lie down while keeping the candle in sight. Breathe deeply and study the candle flame. Chant:

New moon, new start,

You know what's in my heart.

You know just what I need.

Tonight I plant the seed.

Let the candle burn out safely. You can also charge an item such as a piece of jewelry, a statue, a crystal, etc., to serve as a reminder of your attitude of renewal.

Ember Grant

 April 6
Saturday

1st ♈

☾ → ♉ 9:06 am

Color of the Day: Black
Incense of the Day: Sage

Spring-Clean Your Altar

Many people do some form of spring cleaning as the days begin to grow longer. You might have done so around the time of the spring equinox. But did you clean and cleanse your altar? If you have an altar, it is the spiritual center of your home, so you want to make sure you keep it neat and clean and occasionally clear the energy that surrounds it.

Start by doing physical cleaning. Dust anything sitting on the altar, maybe rearranging or adding things if it no longer feels quite right. Then take some incense (citrus or rosemary is good) or a sage smudge stick and waft the smoke around the altar to clear away any lingering negativity or stagnant energy from the winter. Sprinkle a bit of salt and water and say:

This altar is cleared and cleansed for another season of positive magical work. So mote it be.

Deborah Blake

April 7
Sunday

1st ♉

Color of the Day: Gold
Incense of the Day: Marigold

Tarot Numerology

Many of us draw a Tarot card each morning to predict how our day might go. We can combine the meanings of Tarot cards with numerology to get more information. If you don't know much about the magic of numbers, go online to learn what numbers tell us.

Reduce numbers above 9 to one digit. For example, calculate card XIV (Temperance) this way:

$14 = 1 + 4 = 5 = $ change or freedom

(You can look up other meanings as well.) If you want to, you can also add up the letters of the word. Use this chart:

1	2	3	4	5	6	7	8	9
A	B	C	D	E	F	G	H	I
J	K	L	M	N	O	P	Q	R
S	T	U	V	W	X	Y	Z	

Temperance = $2 + 5 + 4 + 7 + 5 + 9 + 1 + 5 + 3 + 5 = 46 = 4 + 6 = 10 = 1 = $ individuality, a new beginning.

If you draw a Minor, use the old, familiar A. E. Waite meaning and also consider the card's number.

Barbara Ardinger

April 8
Monday

1st ♉

☽ v/c 4:29 am
☽ → ♊ 5:15 pm

Color of the Day: Gray
Incense of the Day: Clary sage

Coin Spell

This is a simple prosperity charm to attract and maintain wealth. You will need two coins, a green candle and holder, and some powdered cinnamon.

Arrange the items on your altar. Light the green candle and imagine yourself paying off debts, saving up for a vacation, or buying that special thing you really want. Feel the happiness and freedom you would experience if you had the money you need. Carefully drip green candle wax onto the coins, and while it is still melted, place a dash of cinnamon powder on top. Drip more wax on top of the cinnamon, then press the coins together like a sandwich, trapping the cinnamon—and your prosperity-attracting energy—inside.

Let the candle burn itself out safely. Keep this charm in your wallet or change purse to keep the cash flowing.

Kate Freuler

April 9
Tuesday

1st ♊

Color of the Day: Red
Incense of the Day: Ginger

Cleanse Us with Rain

Blessed be the falling rain, which cleanses, renews, and makes us whole again.

On a morning after a rainfall, step outside. Feel the enchantment of the world washed anew.

Gently wipe the fresh morning rain from the leaves of a tree or the petals of a flower. Touch your forehead, your eyelids, your cheeks, your lips, and the back of your neck with the fresh rain. You may even wish to wipe your throat with the rain. As the water lingers on your skin, feel its refreshing coolness and lightness of being. Take the water energy into your being, just as the leaves take the moisture into the tree. Legends say touching your skin with water from a fresh rain, especially in the morning, keeps your skin healthy, young, and vibrant.

Merge with the power of water that falls from the sky in gentle drops.

Najah Lightfoot

April 10
Wednesday

1st ♊

☽ v/c 1:27 pm

☽ → ♋ 11:31 pm

Color of the Day: Brown
Incense of the Day: Marjoram

Communicate with a Sylph

This spell will assist you in contacting a sylph: an air elemental. Typically, these beings provide clarity of mind, new perspectives, and a general feeling of mental renewal. Invoke them when you feel stuck or are in need of inspiration.

For this spell you will need some resin incense (I prefer black copal), a charcoal-safe incense burner, and some charcoal. Light the charcoal. Ground and center. Face the east, or the direction your tradition associates with the air element. Enter a trance and sprinkle some of the resin on the coal, watching the smoke rise into the air. Call to the sylphs—the conscious beings of the air—to appear in the smoke before you:

Creatures of the very air,

Reveal here to me your form.

Look into the smoke with the Witch's eye: your inner sight. Allow the sylphs to reveal themselves to you. Once they have, you may commune with them as you wish.

Storm Faerywolf

April 11
Thursday

1st ♋

Color of the Day: Crimson
Incense of the Day: Mulberry

A Morning Meditation

April mornings are alive with signs that the earth is awakening from its winter rest. The birds are singing and buds are opening, and silvery dew drops spangle each blade of grass. Many occultists believe that morning dew has magical qualities that trigger psychic and meditative abilities.

On an April morning when you won't be disturbed, go outside. Breathe deeply. Then moisten a finger with dew. Anoint the middle of your forehead with the dew. This will awaken the powers of your third eye. Sit still. Let any images come to you. You may have visions of future events. You might get a "feeling." Or you may slip into a meditative state. Slowly return to your everyday frame of mind. Record your visions/feelings and see what happens. Do this meditation as often as you wish.

James Kambos

NOTES:

April 12
Friday

1st ♋

2nd Quarter 3:06 pm

☽ v/c 7:33 pm

Color of the Day: Pink
Incense of the Day: Cypress

Cerealia Celebration Altar

Cerealia was an ancient Roman festival celebrated at this time of year in honor of the goddess Ceres. She is a goddess of many things, including agriculture, grains, and the harvest. Her domain is fertility, motherhood, and women. Crops are sacred to Ceres. She is a goddess who speaks to the everyday person.

Cerealia was an eight-day festival thought to have begun on or around April 12th. The following altar is inspired by this observance. It promises to enrich your fertility in whatever area you need it.

Ritual and Ceremony

Wearing a white robe or dress, begin setting up your altar at sunrise.

Gather some wheat sheaves and tie them with a simple hemp string.

Create a cornucopia (horn of plenty) out of some fresh, local crops.

Set your wheat sheaves and cornucopia on a green cloth on your altar.

Set out and then light a circle of white candles in holders.

Altar

Reflect on your Cerealia altar at sundown. Bring it your wish for fertility, health, and good living. Be sure to extinguish the candles.

Stephanie Rose Bird

April 13
Saturday

2nd ♋

☽ → ♌ 3:50 am

Color of the Day: Blue
Incense of the Day: Magnolia

A Spell to Destroy Negative Thought Patterns

Sometimes that voice in the back of your head isn't a good thing. Negative thinking can defeat us before we even go to battle, and there is no time like the present to destroy the cycle of negative thoughts!

For this spell you will need to keep a journal with you and log each time you catch yourself spiraling into a negative thought. At the end of the day, light a black candle and place it between you and a mirror, then read each negative thought aloud. After reading each negative thought you must respond with the reason that thought is untrue or unrealistic and then banish it by saying:

I send this thought into the flame.
No more of my life force it can claim!

Repeat this once daily for a week and then again as necessary. Let the candle burn down completely and safely each time.

Devin Hunter

April 14
Sunday

2nd ♌

☽ v/c 9:38 pm

Color of the Day: Amber
Incense of the Day: Heliotrope

Palm Sunday

Spell for Victory

For this spell you'll need a crown or a tiara, which can be purchased from a party supply store or made out of construction paper or vines. You'll also need a blank piece of paper and a pen. On the paper, create an award with your name and an affirmation of the success you're wishing to gain. For instance, if you want a new job, you might design the award to say "In recognition of a job well gained." Place the crown on your head and hold your award proudly in front of you. Stand before a mirror and imagine how you will feel, how you will stand, how you will smile, when you have this success. Carry the award with you or keep it in your home to help manifest your dreams and to help give you the courage to do so.

Melanie Marquis

April 15
Monday

2nd ♌

☽ → ♍ 6:14 am

Color of the Day: Ivory
Incense of the Day: Narcissus

honor the Family

April is an important and busy month in my family, with many births, deaths, and anniversaries. Perhaps there is a month like that in your family. It is a wonder how the planets and the stars, nature, and the universe align and make a particular month so special (or so sad).

We can honor any special/sacred month. Plan celebrations for the living and for those who have passed. You may wish to plan one gathering to celebrate all the birthdays in that month at one time, and during that celebration offer up words for those who have passed. Don't forget to include the god and goddess attached to that month. Say:

In honor of our family:

To those who have gone before, we ask that you keep a watchful eye over us.

To those coming in, bring the love with which you were created.

Emyme

April 16
Tuesday

2nd ♍

Color of the Day: White
Incense of the Day: Cedar

healing and Cleansing with Spring herbs

Many spring herbs are natural detoxifiers, a gift from Mother Nature to help us clear away the sludge of a winter often spent eating fatty comfort foods and not getting enough exercise. Dandelions, nettles, and milk thistle all cleanse the liver and the blood, and as a bonus, nettle is good for allergies, especially if started before the worst of the pollen shows up. If you want to add some magical work to your cleansing, dandelions have been used for divination and making wishes, and nettles are good for protection and healing. Pick young dandelion or nettle leaves and put them on your salad or make a healing tea. For an extra boost, bless the herbs before you use them by saying:

Bless these herbs, gifts of the spring, that they may cleanse my body and spirit.

Deborah Blake

April 17
Wednesday

2nd ♏

☽ v/c 12:29 am

☽ → ♎ 7:22 am

Color of the Day: Topaz
Incense of the Day: Lavender

Invoking Tara Buddha

In Vajrayana Buddhism, Tara is a female incarnation of Buddha and is known as the mother of liberation. Meditating on Tara enables practitioners to develop and understand compassion and emptiness.

Years ago, on April 17, I began labor, and my daughter Terra was born two days later. Parenting is a transcendental path toward compassion and emptiness. I understand the need to protect and nurture my child while simultaneously encouraging her to go farther and longer away, developing independence.

Today, bring to mind one of your babies: a child, a pet, a garden, an artistic creation, or even a car—we baby so much in life. Hold your hands over your heart and draw your baby to mind.

Chant:

Bless you for teaching me compassion.

Thank you for teaching me emptiness.

May Tara Buddha walk with you in liberation as you venture independently into the world, protected from fear, danger, and illness, with increased longevity and prosperity.

Dallas Jennifer Cobb

April 18
Thursday

2nd ♎

Color of the Day: Purple
Incense of the Day: Clove

Grasping Prosperity with Five-Finger Grass

We can all use a bit of extra prosperity from time to time. Here is a lovely little spell to promote that prosperous flow in our lives. Thursday's planetary ruler is Jupiter, and one of my favorite prosperity herbs, cinquefoil (aka five-finger grass), corresponds with Jupiter. Anoint a small green chime candle with olive oil and roll it in a very small amount of cinquefoil. Place in a holder on top of a heatproof dish or inside a cauldron. Sprinkle more cinquefoil around the candleholder. Light the candle and recite the following while visualizing a growing prosperous energy:

Flaming candle, burning bright,

Five-finger grass reaching into the ethers with might,

Grasping prosperity and maintaining flow,

May it continue to grow and grow,

May it be steady in its flow,

For the best, may it be so!

Let the candle burn down safely.

Blake Octavian Blair

April 19
Friday

2nd ♎

☽ v/c 7:12 am
🌕 Full Moon 7:12 am
☽ → ♏ 8:41 am

Color of the Day: Coral
Incense of the Day: Orchid

Good Friday

Family Full Moon Ritual

This is a small, simple ritual we do in my family to honor and acknowledge the full moon. You will need a sheet of paper, a pencil, a handful of your favorite fresh or dried herbs, and a small fire (optional).

On the paper have each person write one thing from the last lunar cycle for which they are thankful or that they wish to change in the coming month. Don't worry if you can't think of any major events. Life is full of small wonders! Place the herbs on top of the writing and carefully fold the paper around them. Take a moment to appreciate the moon together in silence. Let the herbs absorb the power of the words written on the paper. Then have everyone hold a corner of the package and throw it into the fire as one.

If you do not have access to a fire, you can dump the herbs out of the paper and into a shallow hole in the earth and then recycle the paper.

Kate Freuler

April 20
Saturday

3rd ♏

☉ → ♉ 4:55 am

Color of the Day: Brown
Incense of the Day: Pine

Passover begins (at sundown
on April 19)

Free to Be

In my home state of Colorado, April 20th is fondly referred to as "420." On this day Coloradans celebrate their victory for medical, medicinal, and recreational cannabis use. What freedoms have you recently achieved? If you haven't achieved your freedom, how are you working toward it? Use the energy of this day to add fuel to the fire and set yourself free!

Cleanse a red candle with Florida Water. Carve the word *freedom* onto the candle. Anoint the candle with frankincense essential oil. Place the candle in a fireproof holder and set on a fireproof dish. Sprinkle a small amount of angelica root around the base of the candleholder.

Light the candle and focus on your intentions. Once the candle has burned out, gather up the angelica root, toss it into the air, and yell:

I am free!

Najah Lightfoot

April 21
Sunday

3rd ♏

☽ v/c 12:00 am

☽ → ♐ 11:59 am

Color of the Day: Orange
Incense of the Day: Almond

Easter

Easter Abundance

Easter is a time of rebirth and new beginnings. It features many symbols of fertility and prosperity, such as flowers, rabbits, ducks, chickens, and eggs. That makes this an ideal opportunity for abundance magic. Begin by coloring at least a dozen eggs. You can now find kits to make gilded eggs; they include the basic dyes, plus a shimmer powder that looks quite gold over yellow dye. Say a blessing over each egg as you prepare it:

Come, abundance, fill this shell.

May its finder do quite well.

If you wish, you may designate each egg with a different type of abundance, such as financial prosperity, healthy pets/livestock, or a loving home. Then gather the eggs together in a basket filled with green grass, which also symbolizes bounty.

Hide the eggs in the traditional way. As each one is found, it will release its blessing into the right hands.

Elizabeth Barrette

April 22
Monday

3rd ♐

Color of the Day: Silver
Incense of the Day: Rosemary

Earth Day

Earth Day with the Spirits of Place

Today is Earth Day, the celebration of our planet and our responsibility for its health and happiness. Today we look around us and appreciate the beauty and splendor that is everywhere, and we reach out to the spirits that reside within the hidden realms of nature.

As is the tradition, plant a tree today somewhere local. Bring along some milk, honey, and cornmeal and place them near the tree as an offering to the spirits of place. Call to the spirits by saying:

Spirits of place, I pray to you.

Be here now amongst the true.

Come ye, wise ones, do not delay.

I bring gifts to guide your way!

Spend time in silence there, reaching out with your consciousness, asking the spirits what you can do and if there is anything you need to know. Then journal about your experience and continue to build your connection with them.

Devin Hunter

 ## April 23
Tuesday

3rd ♐

☽ v/c 7:44 am

☽ → ♑ 6:50 pm

Color of the Day: Gray
Incense of the Day: Cinnamon

Vinalia Urbana Open-Air Altar

The Vinalia Urbana was a Roman wine festival held on this day in honor of Jupiter and Venus and their qualities of protection, strength, health, love, and happiness.

Pack the following in a shopping bag:

- An annual varietal wine (released spring 2019)
- Corkscrew
- Wine glass
- Charcoal
- Lighter
- Handful dried mint and myrtle
- A small ox icon
- 2 snake toys
- Freshly gathered oak leaves

Pick a hillside, preferably one shielded by a large oak tree. Set out your materials. Set out the ox icon, snakes, and oak leaves as a temporary altar.

Open the wine and pour some in the glass. Say:

Blessings, Mother Earth, from Jupiter.

Pour some wine on the earth. Say:

Blessings, Mother Earth, from Venus.

Pour some wine on the earth. Say:

Blessings, Mother Earth, from me.

Pour some wine on the earth.

Place charcoals inside a fire-safe container, and light them. Sprinkle with the crumbled mint and myrtle.

Look toward the sky, the domain of Jupiter. Ask for what you wish.

After the spell is completed, make your footprint small by cleaning up after yourself. Take your ox and snakes with you, along with the other materials. Let the oak leaves return to Mother Nature.

Stephanie Rose Bird

April 24
Wednesday

3rd ♑

Color of the Day: Yellow
Incense of the Day: Honeysuckle

Guerilla Gardening

When you're out in your neighborhood, do you notice little bare, ugly patches of dirt where nothing is growing? Not everyone honors our mother planet as we do. How can you help Gaia bloom in out-of-the-way places? Guerilla gardening! Bring life to those little patches of dirt by planting and caring for the plants. As you engage in guerilla gardening, any time of the night or day, you may spot other people doing the same holy work.

Identify a bare spot that needs more life. Cast a modest (small, unfancy, invisible) circle and set small rocks (gravel works) in the four cardinal directions. Or draw an invisible pentacle and set rocks on the five points. Now do your planting. Choose easy-care plants like oxalis (shamrock).

Don't abandon your guerilla garden. Water your plants. Keep an eye on them. You're fostering life on our mother planet. Help keep Gaia green.

Barbara Ardinger

April 25
Thursday

3rd ♑

☽ v/c 3:48 pm

Color of the Day: Purple
Incense of the Day: Apricot

The WiFi Witchery Spell

An effective Witch will use whatever tools they have available. Why not put your WiFi signal to (magical) work? These home networks can be named anything, so why not make yours a new type of "sigil" for your long-term goals? What do you want to attract? Money? Opportunity? Health? Protection? Choose a word or short phrase that speaks of this goal and then make this the name of your WiFi network. This will be broadcasted by your router and can be picked up by those around who are looking for a WiFi signal. Making sure you have a strong password, enchant this name to be a beacon that attracts the qualities it represents by placing your hands over the router and saying:

Beacon of invisible light,

Shine your charge between the worlds

And draw to me that which I invite

By name, by sign, by holy words.

Refresh the spell monthly.

Storm Faerywolf

April 26
Friday

3rd ♑

☽ → ♒ 5:27 am

4th Quarter 6:18 pm

Color of the Day: White
Incense of the Day: Mint

Arbor Offering

Today is Arbor Day in the US. Think of all that trees do, are, and provide: shelter, fuel, building materials, shade, oxygen, beauty, paper products, and syrups. In honor of Arbor Day, make an offering to a tree in your area. You'll need a jug of water. Kneel by the tree and say:

Blessed be your roots that
hold this sacred earth.

Pour some water.

Blessed be your leaves that
cleanse our sweet air.

Pour more water.

Blessed be your wood that
feeds our magical fires.

Pour more water.

Blessed be your sap, the water
of your living branches.

Pour more water.

As I lie in your shade or gather
your leaves, I pledge to care
for you as you care for me.

Bring the tree some water occasionally.

Dallas Jennifer Cobb

April 27
Saturday

4th ♒

Color of the Day: Indigo
Incense of the Day: Patchouli

Passover ends

Amulet to Remove Obstacles

This spell can be used to clear obstacles that are preventing you from achieving your goals. If you know what the obstacle is, visualize it. If you don't, then simply imagine yourself achieving your goal unencumbered. Carry this amulet to clear the way. Use a small drawstring bag to create a bundle. Add any combination of frankincense (one grain), sagebrush (three leaves), and a sprig each of mint and rosemary, in addition to four grains of coarse sea salt. Herbs may be fresh or dried.

Choose any combination of stones from this group and charge them for your purpose: dolomite, kunzite, sulfur, or zoisite. Charge the stones by holding them and visualizing your intent. Add a piece of topaz, if you have it. Clear quartz can be substituted for any of the stones.

Chant three times:

Opposition be removed,
my way ahead shall be improved.

Carry the bundle with you as long as necessary.

Ember Grant

▽ **April 28**
Sunday

4th ♒

☽ v/c 5:44 am
☽ → ♓ 6:11 pm

Color of the Day: Yellow
Incense of the Day: Frankincense

Our Lady of Life, Gaia Sophia

To positively impact Gaia Sophia, honor the earth and plant a tree today. Please do your bit in the here and now; shine like the beautiful rainbow-sparkle child of emergent earth consciousness that you are. If we each plant even a handful of trees in our lifetime, then the impact will save earth-based religions such as ours from having no truly wild forests left to draw a circle within.

Think about the power of an old grove of trees, and take a moment to gift or plant a tree or perhaps a shrub. Choose something nice but not too expensive that will thrive on your property, or offer it to a coven or family member who owns land. Let your worship of the earth be at the end of a spade. Let's weave our temples to Gaia Sophia in the woodlands of our living Mother Earth and help to resuscitate our planet.

Estha McNevin

April 29
Monday

4th ♓

Color of the Day: Lavender
Incense of the Day: Hyssop

Dream Divination Spell

On a length of white or purple ribbon, write a question for which you wish to find an answer. Tie this onto your bed frame or slip it inside your pillowcase. Before you fall asleep, state your question and express your intention to gain an answer through your dreams. Keep a notebook and pen handy so that when you wake up, you can write down any impressions that you remember. The answer might come in the form of symbols, images, or metaphors. Repeat this for seven nights or until you gain an answer. If you don't find a satisfactory answer within the week, formulate your question another way and try again.

Melanie Marquis

 April 30
Tuesday

4th ♓
☽ v/c 5:57 pm

Color of the Day: Black
Incense of the Day: Basil

May Eve

Bonfires and revelry! No matter what hemisphere you reside in and what season you are welcoming (the first blush of summer or the last of the harvest), this day, this evening, is a time of celebration. At dusk, gather loved ones around the warmth and the light of a fire pit or fireplace and serve refreshments. Should a fire pit not be an option, you can use candles, of all shapes and sizes. For safety, use those in glass containers, with complementary scents. Add tapers of differing heights, all ranged on a silver or mirrored tray. Feast on seasonal fruits and vegetables and cakes and ale. Music and dancing? Yes, indeed! Chant:

Fire,

Elemental and strong,

Purifying and hypnotizing,

We celebrate your power.

Fire,

Bright light of the gods,

Bring the luck of May

Into this home, this bower.

Emyme

May

Welcome to the famously merry month of May! Though it was originally named after the Greek fertility goddess Maia, the Catholic Church has since designated this month as sacred to the Virgin Mary, even referring to her as "the Queen of May" during this time. Day one of this flower-filled month is the beloved holiday of Beltane, during which the veil that usually conceals the world of the fairies fades, and our power to make contact with them reaches its yearly peak. Indeed, May's birth flower is a fairy favorite: the lily of the valley. As for our skies, this month they host the Eta Aquariids meteor shower, which reaches its peak around May 6 and is most visible before the sunrise.

May is also the month when the light half of the year begins to assert itself in earnest, and we sense the days lengthening, the sun growing warmer, and the leaves filling out the trees. This allows us to gaze bravely into our own brilliance and to courageously release anything that has been holding us back from being our most radiant, expansive, beautiful selves. Indeed, May's bright presence reminds us to claim the vital prosperity that is our birthright and our natural state.

Tess Whitehurst

May 1
Wednesday

4th ♓

☽ → ♈ 6:24 am

Color of the Day: White
Incense of the Day: Bay laurel

Beltane

Flower Spell

Today is Beltane, the celebration of the Great Rite between the God and Goddess. This potted plant craft is inspired by the red and white ribbons of the traditional maypole, and the fertility of this sabbat day is represented by planting a flower.

You will need some red and white tissue paper cut into strips, some flower seeds of your choice, a flowerpot filled with dirt, colorful crayons, and some clear-drying craft glue.

Write blessings or inspirational quotes or draw symbols on the strips of paper with the crayons according to what situations you would like to see grow and take form in your life. Then glue the strips onto the flowerpot in patterns or stripes. When the glue is dry, add the soil to the pot. The soil represents the Goddess and the seeds represent the God. As you press the seeds into the earth, contemplate the union of God and Goddess, the power of creation. Cover the seeds with soil, water regularly, and see what grows!

Kate Freuler

May 2
Thursday

4th ♈

Color of the Day: Crimson
Incense of the Day: Mulberry

Brothers and Sisters Day

This is Brothers and Sisters Day, which honors siblings of blood and spirit, and the special relationship between them. Close platonic ties are often spoken of in this regard. If you don't have any siblings, consider volunteering with Big Brothers Big Sisters of America or a similar organization.

For this spell you will need a picture of something to symbolize siblings. The constellation Gemini, cherry twins, or peas in a pod can all be used. Cast a circle and invoke sibling deities, such as the twins Artemis and Apollo, sisters Pele and Namakaokahai, or brothers in spirit Gilgamesh and Enkidu. Ask them to fill your life with brotherly/sisterly love. Meditate on the sibling bonds in your family of blood and/or choice. Charge the symbol with this energy. Finally, release the deities and your circle.

Afterward, you may keep the symbol on your altar, carry it, or give it to your sibling.

Elizabeth Barrette

May 3
Friday

4th ♈

☽ v/c 4:47 am

☽ → ♉ 4:18 pm

Color of the Day: Pink
Incense of the Day: Yarrow

Threat Containment Spell

If there is a threatening person in your life and you would like some magickal protection to supplement your mundane forms of protection, such as locked doors and restraining orders, try this spell.

You'll need a small scrap of paper, a pen, a black candle, and a resealable jar that's been painted black or covered with black paper. Write the person's name as small as possible on the paper, then set it ablaze (carefully) in the flame of the black candle. Quickly drop it into the jar. Hold the candle above the jar so that the black wax drips onto the paper and ashes, completely covering it. Seal the jar by placing the lid on it as tightly as possible, then throw this away in a dumpster far from your home as you affirm your intention for the person to be out of your life, unable to influence you or harm you.

Melanie Marquis

May 4
Saturday

4th ♉

New Moon 6:45 pm

Color of the Day: Blue
Incense of the Day: Rue

Nimuë's Petals

This is a spell to bless any new project or endeavor and clear away any obstacles to success by invoking Nimuë, the faery goddess of wild innocence and joy.

For this spell you will need six white roses, a vase, a white candle and holder, and a piece of candy.

At the time of the new moon, or later in the evening in the cloak of darkness, take three white roses to a three-way crossroads and reverently tear their petals from the blooms, casting them before you to each road and saying:

As petals tossed upon the wind

Innocent, the winsome heart

Shall bless the paths before me now,

An open road, a fresh new start.

Speak the faery goddess's name aloud three times to each road:

Nimuë! Nimuë! Nimuë!

Return home. Light a white candle before a vase of three white roses and place the piece of candy before it all as an offering. Allow the candle to burn down safely.

Storm Faerywolf

May 5
Sunday

1st ♉

☽ v/c 11:10 am

☽ → ♊ 11:40 pm

Color of the Day: Orange
Incense of the Day: Juniper

Cinco de Mayo

Magical Water

In his book *The Hidden Messages in Water*, Dr. Masuro Emoto demonstrates that water absorbs energy, which changes the molecular structure of the water. Today, make magical water and a magical jar, so you can change the energy you drink in.

You will need a glass jar with a resealable lid, an indelible marker, and water.

Clean and dry the jar. Write *Love* on the lid with the marker. Fill the jar with water.

Wrap your hands around the jar. Draw to mind things you love, raising your love vibration and transferring it to the water. Lean over the jar and whisper:

I love you.

Feel love.

Put the lid on and carry this jar with you, drinking magically charged water regularly. With each sip, drink in the love.

Water can be imprinted with any message. Writing your message on the lid enables the message to be absorbed into your consciousness in a variety of ways.

Dallas Jennifer Cobb

May 6
Monday

1st ♊︎

Color of the Day: Silver
Incense of the Day: Narcissus

Ramadan begins

A Day of Fasting

Today marks the beginning of Ramadan, the ninth month of the Islamic calendar, a time that is spent fasting from dawn until sunset. Muslims also observe this sacred time by saying prayers and doing good deeds. While most of the folks reading this book probably aren't Muslim, all of these things are good for the spirit, so why not take a day to fast in honor of our own sacred spiritual beliefs, say a few extra prayers, and maybe do a good deed or two? Fasting for spiritual reasons (rather than health or diet) should be done with an attitude of reverence. You might want to make a special tea to drink during the day, made from your favorite herbs, and when you break your fast at sunset, eat slowly and mindfully, with gratitude for the food.

Deborah Blake

May 7
Tuesday

1st ♊︎

☽ v/c 7:50 pm

Color of the Day: Gray
Incense of the Day: Geranium

Dandelions and Spirit Contact

Dandelion foliage is a powerful aid in drawing spirits of the deceased. To do this, you'll need a few dandelion leaves that have never been sprayed with weed killer. You will also need some water, a saucepan with a lid, a cloth, and a scrying tool such as a magic mirror.

Boil the water in the saucepan and add the dandelion leaves. Cover the pan and take it off the heat, then let the mixture steep for a few minutes. When the mixture cools, dampen the cloth with it and wipe off the scrying tool you'll use. Set the pan near you and begin to scry. Then say:

Spirit (or deceased's name), come to me.

Come only in love and peace.

When you see the spirit's image, you may ask a question. Then thank the spirit and let it go. Afterward, pour the water and leaves respectfully upon the earth. If you didn't succeed in making contact, try again. Just keep your sessions short.

James Kambos

May 8
Wednesday

1st ♊

☽ → ♋ 5:06 am

Color of the Day: Topaz
Incense of the Day: Honeysuckle

Magickal Medicine

Today, let's boost the power of our intentions by creating a first aid kit infused with the magickal healing properties of essential oils. There are so many from which to choose, so to start, concentrate on just one: clove. Research shows that cloves—whole and ground—have healing properties too numerous to mention here. Dental problems and headaches are just two of the issues that clove oil can help heal. After brushing, swish your mouth with clove oil and salt well diluted in water. Clove oil mixed with salt and applied to the forehead or the base of the neck can ease the pain of headaches. When using clove oil, be sure to follow all the precautions, as it can burn the skin when applied at full strength. For more healing ideas, see organicfacts.net.

Emyme

May 9
Thursday

1st ♋

☽ v/c 10:06 pm

Color of the Day: White
Incense of the Day: Balsam

Our Lord of Light, IAO Pan

If we want to leave behind the doldrums of winter and surpass the storms of spring, we have to look to the sweet promise of summer. This spell is sure to bring the name of Pan to your lips all season as you revel in the unbridled glory and light of regeneration. Find a private, sunny location and place a one-pound container of honey on top of a gold ring or amulet. Clap and slap the earth rhythmically as you chant:

IAO Pan!

Be sure to act like a kid: roll all around, gesticulating your jazz hands enthusiastically to consecrate the honey with vigorous solar energy. While you perform this wild celebration of spring, charge the honey with life in the golden and glowing light of the day. Revel in the light with wild abandon. Draw the spirit of the wildwood to bless your enchanted honey with radiance as you cry out:

O, god of nature!

Estha McNevin

May 10
Friday

1st ♋

☽ → ♌ 9:14 am

Color of the Day: Rose
Incense of the Day: Orchid

Garden Protection Spell

If you keep a garden or even just a few houseplants, use this spell to protect them and to encourage healthy, flourishing growth. This spell can be used for any type of plant, indoor or out.

Visualize your plants in perfect health; picture the ideal growing conditions. Imagine an invisible protective shell or bubble around the plants that allows air, light, and water to enter but repels anything harmful, such as pests and disease. Add a quartz crystal to the bed or pot, if desired, as an added protective measure. Chant:

Roots grow deep, and branches strong, growing season full and long.

Bless this garden and its yield, protect it with a magic shield.

Let no weather, pest, or blight harm these plants, day or night.

Ember Grant

 May 11
Saturday

1st ♌

2nd Quarter 9:12 pm

Color of the Day: Indigo
Incense of the Day: Sandalwood

Lemuria Spell for Ancestors and Spirits

Lemuria is an ancient Roman festival that was held on May 9, 11, and 13. This is the time when a ceremony like the Day of the Dead occurred. The following spell is designed to keep evil ghost spirits of all stripes at bay while also feeding your ancestors.

Begin by taking off your shoes. There shouldn't be any knots in your clothing either. Walking barefoot wards off evil.

Gather and wash nine black beans in spring water.

Put a cleansed and dry black bean in your mouth. Focus on the work at hand. When ready, spit it over your shoulder. Do not look back.

Incant:

This I cast;

With these beans, I redeem me and mine!

Repeat this action eight more times (for a total of nine times), each time with a fresh bean.

Stephanie Rose Bird

May 12
Sunday

2nd ♌

☽ v/c 8:24 am

☽ → ♍ 12:22 pm

Color of the Day: Gold
Incense of the Day: Hyacinth

Mother's Day

Offering to Mother Earth

On Mother's Day, it's important to remember to honor Mother Earth, our first mother. Think of a natural feature local to you that you find sacred, such as a stream, a large wall of exposed rock, or a special tree in your yard. These features, while having individual spirits, are also manifestations and parts of the body of our Mother Earth. Gather some eco-friendly offerings for Mother Earth in a small basket or on a tray with a small bell or rattle. Reverently approach your chosen natural feature. Ring the bell or shake the rattle to announce your presence, and petition the spirits and Mother Earth. Sprinkle the offerings at the base of your chosen feature. Offer a prayer, such as the following:

Mother Earth, I ask thee,

Help me live more gently.

*My gratitude to you and
all your creatures.*

May they be our sacred teachers.

Blake Octavian Blair

May 13
Monday

2nd ♍

Color of the Day: Ivory
Incense of the Day: Hyssop

Birds, Bats, Butterflies & Bees

Is anything more magical than flying? Though Icarus tried it, modern people had to invent the airplane. But we can fly in our imagination! Using visualization, we can fly to celebrate sabbats and do magic with other circles and covens, or we can go online and "fly" to a website for a web-wide ritual. When you want to fly, speak this invocation (apologies to Percy Bysshe Shelley):

Hail to thee, blithe flyer,

Higher still and higher

From the earth thou springest

Like a cloud of fire:

The blue deep thou wingest,

*And singing still dost soar,
and soaring ever singest.*

In these days of climate change and increased pollution, the multitudes of winged species need our protection. We've all read how honeybees are dying. Sign petitions addressed to manufacturers and stores asking them to stop making and selling pesticides containing neonicotinoids, and plant flowers that attract our winged friends.

Barbara Ardinger

May 14
Tuesday

2nd ♏

☽ v/c 1:19 pm

☽ → ♎ 2:51 pm

Color of the Day: Red
Incense of the Day: Ylang-ylang

Mars Spell for New Beginnings

On Tuesday, Mars rules the heavens and brings with it the power to initiate new beginnings. Today, take a red candle and inscribe the acronym NWBGN (for New Beginning) on it. Light it while facing the east and say:

Earth to Mars, Earth to Mars,
transmitting now across the stars!

Earth to Mars, Earth to Mars,
transmitting now across the stars!

From my mind to your will,
I summon now the Martian skill.

From your palace you now spill,
here this candle you now fill.

In its direction you now flow,
toward its path you now go.

With your blessing let it grow,
with your passion make it so!

Create the mental image of you successfully embarking on the new beginning and then project it into the east. Let the candle burn out completely and safely, then place the remnants in a red cloth pouch, along with some nettle, hyssop, and rue, and place on your altar.

Devin Hunter

May 15
Wednesday

2nd ♎

Color of the Day: Brown
Incense of the Day: Marjoram

Brew a Cuppa

Our first sip in the morning is precious. The first sip warms our hearts and galvanizes our minds into action. After our first cup, we are ready for the day.

But before you take that first sip, why not pause and give thanks to the earth for providing your delicious tea or coffee? It can be hard to wait, to step back a moment, before your lips touch the cup. But the reward is worth it.

Brew your morning libation with the intention of giving gratitude to the earth. If possible, step outside and raise your cup to the east. Bring your cup to your nose. Smell the essence of the tea or coffee beans and say:

Thank you for this blessed coffee (or tea). I share my first drink with thee.

Pour a small amount of your drink onto the earth. Sip, drink, and be merry!

Najah Lightfoot

May 16
Thursday

2nd ♎

☽ v/c 5:37 am
☽ → ♏ 5:26 pm

Color of the Day: Green
Incense of the Day: Apricot

Wealth Magnification Spell

Take three dollar bills and stand with them before a mirror. Count the bills in your hands, and count the bills you see reflected in the mirror. Imagine a whole series of mirrors, your dollars reflected on each surface. Tuck the dollars into your pocket as you say:

The more I give, the more will come!
A thousand strong will be each
one! The currency will flow to me,
from me to you, then back to me!

Spend the dollars in different places or give them to friends or strangers. Money will be drawn to you, and your wealth will be magnified.

Melanie Marquis

May 17
Friday

2nd ♏

Color of the Day: Pink
Incense of the Day: Alder

Key Employment Spell

One of the biggest hurdles in finding the right job can be what seems to be a lack of options or opportunities. This key charm is meant to open the doors of opportunity and attract desirable job prospects into your life.

Find a key that you are certain has actually been used to open a door or a lock. Avoid ornamental keys or jewelry charms—a real key is best. Put the key on a length of string or chain. On the side of an orange candle, carve or write the world *opportunity*. Light the candle. As you imagine yourself working the kind of job you desire, carefully hold the key in the candle flame until it is hot. Let the flame fill it up with power, and visualize doors opening up all around you.

Once the key has cooled completely, wear it around your neck or carry it with you. Keep your eyes and ears open for perfect opportunities.

Kate Freuler

May 18
Saturday

2nd ♏

☽ v/c 5:11 pm

Full Moon 5:11 pm

☽ → ♐ 9:21 pm

Color of the Day: Black
Incense of the Day: Rue

healing Affirmation

We all need healing from time to time, whether it is physical, mental, or spiritual. Use this affirmation whenever you need a boost.

I am stronger than I think,

Stronger than I feel,

Rooted in the earth,

Cleansed by the air,

Inspired by the fire,

Healed by the water.

I am stronger than I think,

And I am healing.

Deborah Blake

May 19
Sunday

3rd ♐

Color of the Day: Amber
Incense of the Day: Eucalyptus

Boundary Vines Druidic Spell

Druids are famous for working with trees, but they also worked with smaller plants. Their sacred bushes and vines included brambles or blackberries, gorse, heather, and ivy. Some species such as hawthorn, hazelnut, holly, and willow can grow either as trees or as bushes. Now is a good time to charm your garden. If you don't have one, you can do someone else's or part of your yard or a park.

For this spell you will need long vines or thin stems, such as willow twigs or blackberry canes. Lay them around the garden's edge to cast the circle. Then put your hands on the earth and chant:

Cerridwen, goddess of death and birth,

Cerridwen, goddess of grain and earth,

Banish the bad and don't let it in,

Gather the good and keep it within.

Visualize the land nourishing your garden but pests being unable to enter. Afterward, leave the stems behind.

Elizabeth Barrette

May 20
Monday

3rd ♐

☽ v/c 1:05 pm

Color of the Day: White
Incense of the Day: Rosemary

Victoria Day (Canada)

A Veil of Constellations

Drawing your birth chart on a ritual veil is a wonderful way to get to know your astrology better. Choose a lightweight cotton-blend scarf and, using a t-shirt pen, begin by carefully drawing the wheel of the zodiac. Using your chart as a reference, mark each zodiac, planet, and house relationship. Be sure to include aspects such as conjunctions, trines, squares, and oppositions.

When your veil is complete, anoint it with orange flower water or oil. Bless it in the sunlight and moonlight of your birthday. This will charge it completely with your astrological energy signature, creating a star print. Veils are great tools for remote healing or red tent work. When worn ceremonially, this shroud can help us to better carry the weight of our karma. Such veils can also become treasured heirlooms for our families and coven members, should they wish to honor or remember us after we have passed on.

Estha McNevin

May 21
Tuesday

3rd ♐

☽ → ♑ 3:56 am

☉ → ♊ 3:59 am

Color of the Day: Maroon
Incense of the Day: Bayberry

What Would You Do with a Windfall?

Your spells and castings for prosperity have provided that which you requested. Sharing is the best way to show gratitude, no matter how the money came to you. Water is necessary for life, so think about ripples in a pond. At home: is there a family member struggling with an expense? Pay it. In the local community: is there a local cause that attracts you? Donate. In your larger community (state/province): seek out volunteer organizations, and send a check. In your country: what natural disasters or humanmade tragedies have recently occurred? Contribute via an internet funding page. If you wish, research the many global nonprofits and commit part of your newfound wealth to them as well.

Naturally, pay your own bills first. It's not good to give if it keeps you in debt. And give what you can. Do not overextend—that negates all the positive energy with which you began.

Chant:

Universe, Creator/Creatrix,
Lord & Lady, Goddess, Gaia:

My spirit overflows with gratitude
at the abundance provided.

Allow me to share, and guide my hand
in the distribution of this wealth.

Freely given, do not hold, all good
comes back to me threefold.

Emyme

May 22
Wednesday

3rd ♑

☽ v/c 11:58 pm

Color of the Day: Yellow
Incense of the Day: Lilac

Creativity Spell

Today is the birthday of some notable people, including the renowned American artist Mary Cassatt (whose paintings often showed the bond between mother and child) and British writer Arthur Conan Doyle, best known for creating the character of Sherlock Holmes. These two could not be more different, but what they have in common is that they followed their passion, and the work that resulted touched many others along the way.

Are you following your own passion? Today, do something creative, whether it is art, cooking, or even crafting a beautiful altar. Here is a simple spell to help. Light a yellow candle and say:

Spirit of air, help me be creative

In whichever way best expresses my heart and soul

And touches others in positive ways.

Let me create beauty in the world

Or simply walk my path to joy.

So mote it be.

Deborah Blake

May 23
Thursday

3rd ♑

☽ → ♒ 1:49 pm

Color of the Day: Turquoise
Incense of the Day: Carnation

A Travel Spell

With the warm weather upon us, many of us will be traveling by car. This spell calls upon Hermes, the ancient Greek god of travel and highways, to protect your car. First find a rock that appeals to you along a road; this is one of the god's symbols. Rub a drop of olive oil on the rock as you call upon Hermes:

Protect me, Hermes, as I travel here, as I travel there.

Protect me as I travel near, as I travel far.

Hermes, protect all who travel in my car.

So mote it be.

Keep this rock in your car at all times. Renew the spell once a year.

James Kambos

May 24
Friday

3rd ♒

Color of the Day: Coral
Incense of the Day: Cypress

Meditation on the Earth Element

This meditation is intended to help you reconnect with the qualities of the earth element, which is nurturing, grounding, fertile, and stable. Focus on whichever qualities are most needed for you at this time, for example, prosperity or healing.

Find objects for your altar that represent the earth element. Plants, flowers, stones, or statues of animals are all good choices. As you meditate upon the object(s) of your choice, invite the power of the earth element using this chant:

Field, flower, tree, and stone,
every part of earth is home.

Nurture spirit, flesh and bone,
remind us we are not alone.

To reinforce the connection, plant something in your garden or buy a potted plant as a reminder of the earth element in your life.

Ember Grant

May 25
Saturday

3rd ♒

☽ v/c 8:51 am

Color of the Day: Brown
Incense of the Day: Ivy

Van Van Spiritual Floor Wash

In New Orleans–style Hoodoo, there is a potent and popular magickal oil called Van Van. It smells of the lemongrass it contains. Typically, it also contains pyrite, also called fool's gold. Van Van oil has many purposes, including protection, clearing, luck, opening the way, abundance, and strength. This is a useful oil to add to your oeuvre of magickal potions, whatever your magickal path.

Van Van floor wash is a way to blend oil and water to fortify, clear, and protect your home, studio, or business. To a bucket of rainwater, add as many drops of Van Van oil as needed to give it a nice smell.

Set your intention for one of Van Van's many qualities to imbue your space.

After sweeping the floor and ridding it of debris, use a mop to wash the floor with your Van Van spiritual floor wash.

Blessed be!

Stephanie Rose Bird

May 26
Sunday

3rd ♒

☽ → ♓ 2:08 am

4th Quarter 12:34 pm

Color of the Day: Gold

Incense of the Day: Almond

Starting a Magickal Journal

This is the anniversary of the death of Samuel Pepys in 1703. He was a member of the English parliament and navy; however, he is best known for the diary he kept, which was later published.

We can apply Pepys's legacy to our personal spiritual practices. As a part of our practice, most of us keep a spiritual journal. If you already do so, today is a good time to consecrate and prepare or start a fresh one. If you do not yet keep a magickal journal, today is an opportunity to begin.

Take a blank journal and your favorite anointing oil or holy water, and stand before your altar. Hold the book to your third eye, beam your intent for the use of this journal into it, and then say a dedication of your choice while anointing the book down its spine. Place the journal on your altar to charge, then make an entry!

Blake Octavian Blair

May 27
Monday

4th ♓

Color of the Day: Gray

Incense of the Day: Lily

Memorial Day

A Toast to the Fallen Warriors

Memorial Day in the United States is devoted to the fallen members of the armed services. This spell calls out to their spirits to ask for protection, for as they served in life, so do many of them serve from beyond the veil. You will need a piece of unlined paper and a pen, flowers in a vase, three candles (red, white, and blue) and holders, and a beverage in a cup for offering.

On the paper draw a large pentacle representing the five branches of the armed forces. Put this and the flowers on your altar, then place the candles and holders in the center of the pentacle. Light, in order, the red, white, and blue candles while saying:

By valor,

By innocence,

By justice,

Let the light of freedom shine,

And let the fallen be nourished and fed.

Make your offering of a beverage to the spirits. Ask them to protect your house and family. Allow the candles to burn down safely.

Storm Faerywolf

May 28
Tuesday

4th ♓

☽ v/c 12:21 am

☽ → ♈ 2:32 pm

Color of the Day: Scarlet
Incense of the Day: Cedar

Plant Spirit Connection

Spring is in full swing and the time has come for the plant kingdom to reign supreme once again. The veil that separates the world of the green ones and our own is thin, making it a perfect time to reach out and meet some new allies.

Spend some time in nature today or with a plant that you have been wanting to spiritually connect with. Reach out with your consciousness and find the vibration of the plant/environment and then allow it to harmonize with your own. When you feel the energy become harmonious with your own, ask that it reveal to you the spirit associated with that vibration. Allow the presence to manifest in your mind's eye and then proceed to introduce yourself and discuss your related magical goals. When you are finished, make an offering of milk and honey to the spirit.

Devin Hunter

May 29
Wednesday

4th ♈

Color of the Day: Topaz
Incense of the Day: Lavender

Celebrating the Oceans

Celebrate the great planetary oceans with this spell. If you live close to the ocean, go to the beach. If you live near a river or stream that (eventually) flows into the ocean, go to it or put a map of it (showing its mouth) on your altar. If you live inland, spread a map of the oceans on your altar. On top of the map, set "seawater" in the biggest, bluest glass bowl you can find. Put toy fish in the bowl if you want to, and little sailboats, too. Then make a wreath of real flowers and leaves (nothing artificial) and stand beside the water or before your altar. Sing this song:

Great Neptune rules over the ocean,

Yamanja rules over the sea.

O, you who have care of our waters,

Bring back your clean water to me.

Bring back, bring back,

Bring back your clean water to us.

(Repeat.)

Set your wreath afloat on the water.

Barbara Ardinger

May 30
Thursday

4th ♈

☽ v/c 11:08 am

Color of the Day: Purple
Incense of the Day: Nutmeg

We Will Burn No More

On this day in 1431, Joan of Arc was burned at the stake. She was burned as a heretic for her unwavering belief and conviction that she could speak directly to God, which was considered heresy in her time. As Witches and Pagans, we can deeply empathize with being persecuted for our beliefs and still grieve for those who were burned at the stake for practicing Witchcraft and falsely accused of heretical acts.

Light a white candle and stand beneath the stars. From your heart, speak your truth to those who have gone before, for those burned at the stake. Tell them you are living proof that they did not die in vain. Sprinkle dried roses on the ground in a circle, and allow your candle to burn out inside the ring of roses. Once the candle has burned out safely, let the wind carry the roses away.

Najah Lightfoot

May 31
Friday

4th ♈

☽ → ♉ 12:43 am

Color of the Day: White
Incense of the Day: Vanilla

Spell to Get Rid of a Deadbeat

Has your college roommate landed on your doorstep and he won't leave? Or does your brother-in-law flop on your sofa for five days and guzzle all your beer? Get rid of these moochers with this spell.

You'll need a piece of paper, a pen, a ritual knife, and some salt. When possible, go into a quiet room and write these words on the paper:

You who won't pay your fair share,

*You whose presence I can
no longer bear,*

*You who've overstayed
your unwanted stay,*

Be gone, be out, be on your way!

Next, point your ritual knife in their direction and quietly speak the words aloud. When done, sprinkle some salt over the words and crumple the paper. Throw it in a trash can away from your home. That should send the deadbeat packing! They'll soon leave.

James Kambos

June

The month of June is a time that inspires warmth, love, passion, and deep appreciation of beauty. Agricultural festivals in old Europe acknowledge and celebrate the many flowers and fruits that become abundant at this time. It is no coincidence that these plants—such as roses, raspberries, strawberries, wildflowers, and those that feature red or pink flowers or fruit—are associated with the planet Venus and the goddess Aphrodite. June is also the traditional month for weddings, and the term *honeymoon* refers to the beverage mead, made from fermented honey, that was traditionally given to the bride and groom as an aphrodisiac.

June brings the start of summer, and for thousands of years the summer solstice has been a prominent festival in many cultures. This celestial festival signifies the beginning of warm weather and abundant growth yet also reminds us of its opposite calendar festival: the winter solstice. All hail the Holly King! Spells done in June are often connected to love, romance, growth, health, and abundance.

Peg Aloi

June 1
4th ♉ **Saturday**

☽ v/c 6:53 pm

Color of the Day: Gray
Incense of the Day: Magnolia

Juno's Spell

June is named for Juno, and the first day of each month is dedicated to her, the Roman queen of the gods. The daughter of Saturn, wife and sister of Jupiter, and mother of Mars, Juno knows a lot about successful relationships. The goddess of marriage, love, and partnership, she is also the guardian spirit of all women.

Invoke Juno's protection and blessing. Draw a warm bath and add seven drops of rose essential oil. Light a candle. Close the door. Bathe reverentially, massaging the fragrant water into your skin. Petition Juno:

I implore thee to protect and guide me,

Bless my mind, spirit, heart, and body,

Help me maintain and build my wealth,

Grow fertile gardens,
relationships, and health.

Extinguish the candle when you are done with your bath. As you dress, know that like the rose oil, Juno cloaks you in protection and blessing. Repeat this spell, as needed, on Juno's day, the first of each month.

Dallas Jennifer Cobb

June 2
4th ♉ **Sunday**

☽ → ♊ 7:48 am

Color of the Day: Amber
Incense of the Day: Heliotrope

Drawing Love Closer to You

For this spell, collect ten pink stones that traditionally signify love. Write the name of the one you desire and your own name as one long "word" (no spaces) on a sheet of pink paper. Lay this on your altar and surround it with the ten pink stones.

Cover the linked names with Tarot card X, the Wheel of Fortune (which is always turning), from your favorite deck.

On the paper, copy Hamlet's love letter to Ophelia in your own handwriting:

Doubt thou the stars are fire,

Doubt that the sun doth move,

Doubt truth to be a liar,

But never doubt I love.

As you move both hands in a deosil (clockwise) circle over your altar, read Hamlet's love letter aloud. At the same time, visualize a warm, loving energy surrounding your desired one and inspiring him or her to think of you. Invite your desired one to come visit you.

Barbara Ardinger

June 3
Monday

4th ♊
New Moon 6:02 am

Color of the Day: White
Incense of the Day: Clary sage

New Moon Reboot

Throughout the course of the year, we all need to stop, take stock of our lives, reassess, and reboot. This new moon, as we head into summer, is the perfect time to check in on the growth of all the things you planted earlier in the year. Is everything going as you'd hoped? If not, what would you change? Make a list or simply focus on what you'd like to go differently from this point on. Then go outside if you can (or sit inside and look out at the darkness), light a white candle, and give yourself a surge of new energy as you say:

New moon, bring me new energy.

Set me on a new path or redirect the old

So that I might move toward positive results.

Progress, prosperity, healing, and balance.

So mote it be.

Deborah Blake

 June 4
Tuesday

1st ♊
☽ v/c 11:42 am
☽ → ♋ 12:17 pm

Color of the Day: Red
Incense of the Day: Geranium

Ramadan ends

Old Maids No More

A quaint newspaper article from June 4, 1953, heralded this day as "Old Maid's Day" in honor of all unmarried women over the age of thirty. We've come a long way. In the modern triumvirate of maiden/mother/crone, a woman at thirty may still be firmly lodged in the maiden years. Celebrate the maidens in your life in a special way. Plan a meal or an outing. Send flowers or an edible bouquet. If you are a maiden, take time to celebrate the mothers and crones in your life. Remember, they were once maidens like you.

Emyme

June 5
Wednesday

1st ♋

Color of the Day: Brown
Incense of the Day: Honeysuckle

Eeny, Meeny, Miny, Moe

Fate and chance are always locked in a heated game of fortuitous happenstance. If you seek an instant answer of any kind today, might I recommend a timeless and classic playground divination method to set your life awhirl with chance and synchronicity?

While not all versions of this rhyme are innocent, the version I recommend and often use is as Scottish as my ancestry. I love using this rhyme from my childhood as a method of exercising chance, whether it be encouraging myself to take a new route home or select a random flavor of ice cream. It's easy: as you chant, eliminate any options that land on *out* and *naught* until only one single option remains. This method rarely disappoints.

Eetle, ottle, black bottle,

Eetle, ottle, out!

If you want bannock and coddle,

Needle me, noddle naught!

This or that black bottle (poison),

This or that is out!

If you want pancakes and indulgent cuddles,

Irritate my head not.

Estha McNevin

June 6
Thursday

1st ♋

☽ v/c 10:10 am

☽ → ♌ 3:16 pm

Color of the Day: Green
Incense of the Day: Clove

Pledge for Fidelity

June is a popular month for weddings, so this ritual can be used for a handfasting ceremony or simply any time two people want to commemorate or renew their bond. All you need for this ritual is an ivy plant or two. Traditionally used for good luck, protection, and fidelity, ivy is often carried by brides. Simply exchange your ivy with another person as you speak the chant together. You can use potted plants, pieces of vine, or even single leaves. The benefit of using potted plants is that you can keep them in your home or plant them in your garden. Here is the chant:

For loyalty and love,

This tenacious vine,

Holding fast in place,

While continuing to climb.

Leaf of love and strength,

Mark this sacred time.

Today we make a pledge

Blessed by the divine.

Ember Grant

 June 7
Friday

1st ♌

Color of the Day: Pink
Incense of the Day: Violet

Rune and a Rose with Freya

Friday is Freya's Day. The Norse goddess Freya wears many hats. Aside from being a mother figure, she also oversees rune lore, prophecy, magick, and love. This makes her a pretty desirable goddess to ask for advice on relationships.

Today, acquire a rose and offer it to Freya. Then, holding a bag, bowl, or box of runes, ask the runes and Freya for guidance on one of your life's relationships. Then reach in, grab three runes, and cast them. If you're not yet versed in the runes, you can find a book or a reliable internet guide to assist in your interpretation of their message. Be sure to journal the results of your readings to refer back to as time passes and events unfold. Repeat this ritual (with an offering) as you feel necessary in the future.

Blake Octavian Blair

June 8
Saturday

1st ♌

☽ v/c 5:23 pm

☽ → ♍ 5:45 pm

Color of the Day: Blue
Incense of the Day: Patchouli

Spirit Guide Oil

Our spirit guides are always with us, but sometimes it isn't easy to sense them. Blend this oil during the daylight hours to bring clarity and enhance communication between you and your spirit guides. Once all the ingredients have been mixed and you have said the enchantment, allow this oil to steep for three days somewhere dark and cool before using for best results.

Mix two parts sage essential oil, two parts lavender essential oil, and one part mugwort essential oil into five parts carrier oil (such as almond or fractionated coconut oil). As you blend the oils together, enchant the mixture by saying:

*Spirit guides and allies, hear my voice
and be here now. May this oil bear
your mark and connect us across
time, matter, energy, and space! May
my thoughts be your thoughts, my
words your words! So must it be!*

Devin Hunter

June 9
Sunday

1st ♍

Color of the Day: Yellow
Incense of the Day: Marigold

**Shavuot (begins at sundown
on June 8)**

The Day of the Holy Book

Today is Shavuot, the Jewish festival that commemorates the delivery of their holy book, the Torah, to the Hebrew tribes at Mount Sinai. It also signals the grain harvest. We Pagans are not cultural pirates; we don't steal other people's rituals. But we can share their remembrance by creating rituals of our own with similar intentions.

Let us therefore look at books we consider holy in a practical sense. We've all been given books or come upon books that changed our lives. Or maybe they "flew" off shelves and landed in our hands. Maybe the book introduced us to the Goddess, maybe it gives Neopagan practices, maybe it's historical, or maybe it's a modern novel.

Bring your covenmates together today, all with their own "holy books." Give thanks to the authors of the books, then read a few specially meaningful paragraphs aloud to each other. What did you "harvest" from your book?

Barbara Ardinger

June 10
Monday

1st ♏

2nd Quarter 1:59 am

☽ v/c 8:01 am

☽ → ♎ 8:29 pm

Color of the Day: Lavender

Incense of the Day: Hyssop

A Strawberry Love Spell

Fresh strawberries, which can be found in many areas at this time of year, should be used for this spell. Strawberries are ruled by Venus, which makes them the perfect love food to serve your romantic partner. First, decide how you wish to serve the strawberries. As you prepare them, say this charm:

Strawberries, sacred food of Venus,

*Protect our love, let nothing
come between us.*

*For you, I prepare this fruit,
the color of sweetest wine,*

*For always I am yours,
and you are mine.*

*From my loving hands to
your passionate lips,*

*May this fruit light the flame
of desire you can't resist.*

Serve this fruit of passion and love on the prettiest dishes you have. If you need an extra bit of punch—in other words, lust—garnish the strawberries with a sprig of fresh mint. As an alternative, you could serve strawberries dipped in chocolate.

James Kambos

June 11
Tuesday

2nd ♎

Color of the Day: Maroon
Incense of the Day: Bayberry

A Grounding Charm

A foundational component of a traditional witch's praxis is that of oneiric (dream) travel. One potential danger of this type of work is the gradual inability to remain grounded and focused. For this reason, it can be useful to create a charm whose purpose is to act as a physical anchor that can assist us in coming back from in between the worlds after our astral travels as well as align our altars toward the manifestation of our magical workings.

For this spell you will need:

- Some black thread
- A piece of iron, such as a nail or railroad spike
- Patchouli oil
- Some sea salt

Ground and center. Wind the thread around the iron while you chant:

Iron in the planet's heart,

Iron in my blood and bones.

Continue until a significant portion of the iron is covered in thread. Anoint with the oil and place in a circle of salt for seven days. Keep this charm on your altar or carry it with you. Hold it after engaging in heavy astral or trance work or whenever you are feeling ungrounded or spacey.

Storm Faerywolf

June 12
Wednesday

2nd ♎

☽ v/c 11:15 am

Color of the Day: Topaz
Incense of the Day: Bay laurel

Dandelion happiness Spell

Bright yellow dandelions grow in abundance in early summer, and although many people consider them weeds, there's no denying the cheerful, sunny flower's association with spring, hope, and fresh starts. When dandelions start to bloom merrily all around us, it's a signal that warmth, growth, and months of sunshine are soon to come.

On a sunny day, pluck a dandelion from somewhere in your neighborhood, hold it over your heart, and say:

Dandelion, dandelion,

Sunshine flower,

Bring me happiness,

Joy, and power.

Warm my soul

And brighten my heart.

Lift my spirits,

Let good times start!

Press the flower against the sidewalk and draw a happy face with it. If you press hard enough it will make a visible yellow mark, but just drawing in the air is fine too. Everyone who walks over the happy face should feel a cheerful vibe in their step.

Kate Freuler

June 13
Thursday

2nd ♎

☽ → ♏ 12:02 am

Color of the Day: Purple
Incense of the Day: Myrrh

Safe Travels Spell

Malachite is a lucky and protective stone for travelers. If you're going on a journey, prepare a piece of malachite beforehand by putting it in the most comfortable or favored place in your home. Let it stay there for a day or two so that it will pick up these energies of home. As you pack for your adventure, place the malachite in your suitcase or backpack and think about the stone returning home safely at the end of your travels. If you're traveling by car, you can place the malachite in the glove compartment or in the trunk of your vehicle.

Melanie Marquis

June 14
Friday

2nd ♏

☽ v/c 3:46 pm

Color of the Day: Rose
Incense of the Day: Thyme

Flag Day

Fire Magick

The following rite utilizes the symbolic nature of the colors of our flag. It incorporates Hoodoo as well, with its use of High John the Conqueror root. High John is thought to be named after an African prince brought to the US and enslaved. Quickly he regained his freedom. This root is beloved because of its connection to freedom and strength. It also serves as a protective shield.

For this rite, soak a High John the Conqueror root in holy oil (olive oil) for one cycle of the moon, or purchase a ready-made version of the oil.

Dress a red, a white, and a blue column candle with your High John the Conqueror oil. Start at the center of each candle and stroke upward. Then go back to the middle and stroke the oil downward.

- Red symbolizes courage, blood, and valor.

- White is for peace and purity.

- Blue represents freedom, peace, and perseverance.

Set the three candles on a fireproof plate. Light them, and as they burn, focus on the qualities of each color. Extinguish the candles when done.

Stephanie Rose Bird

 June 15
Saturday

2nd ♏

☽ → ♐ 5:03 am

Color of the Day: Indigo
Incense of the Day: Sandalwood

Darling Dandelion

A dandelion is an original potherb, which is an old name for "vegetable." European immigrants who weren't sure of what type of food might be here when they arrived brought dandelions to the United States. A dandelion is a complete source of nutrition. Dandelion leaves are high in minerals and vitamins and can be used in salads or eaten raw. A dandelion root cleaned, roasted, and ground is a good coffee substitute. There is also the famous dandelion wine, for which recipes can be found with a simple online search.

So the next time you see a dandelion "weed" sprouting in your yard, take a moment before you pull it and realize how valuable this yellow flower was to immigrants. If you're lucky enough to see a dandelion puffball intact, bend down, make a wish, and blow your wishes to the sky!

Najah Lightfoot

June 16
Sunday

2nd ♐

Color of the Day: Gold
Incense of the Day: Juniper

Father's Day

honoring the Divine Masculine

This is Father's Day, a time to celebrate male parents. It's also a great opportunity for honoring the divine masculine. Pagan faiths have many different gods that you can explore.

For this spell you will need a brown candle in a candleholder that you can carry safely. Light it and invoke your favorite divine father figure. Meditate on all that a father brings to a home, and what a father god brings to his pantheon. Then walk through all the rooms of your house. Light them up with the glow of his regard. As you go, say:

Father God, guard my home,

And keep us safe and well.

Make this place full of love

And good stories to tell.

Return the candle to the altar. Finish with favorite remembrances of your father or another male role model. Then give your thanks and let the candle burn out safely.

Elizabeth Barrette

 June 17
Monday

2nd ♐

☽ v/c 4:31 am

Full Moon 4:31 am

☽ → ♑ 12:13 pm

Color of the Day: Silver
Incense of the Day: Lily

Tarot Contemplation

Today is a full moon. The Moon card in the tarot often appears to ask us to look where we may be encountering illusions in our lives. Perhaps things aren't exactly as they seem. Maybe there are fears that need to be confronted.

Tonight, take the image of the Moon card that you'd like to meditate on from a tarot deck and head outside with it in hand. Find a spot to sit comfortably for a short while you gaze at the moon. Looking at the moon and your card, glancing between them as needed for direction, energy, and inspiration, contemplate and meditate on areas in your life where you feel you're confused or unclear. Ask Grandmother Moon for guidance. When you feel strongly inspired, you probably have at least the beginning of your answers. Head inside and journal your thoughts. Review your notes as you work through these areas in your life.

Blake Octavian Blair

June 18
Tuesday

3rd ♑

Color of the Day: Scarlet
Incense of the Day: Cinnamon

National Splurge Day

Splurge, spend, spree! Taking
into consideration your financial
circumstances, today is the day to
splurge on yourself. Is there some
tool or instrument for your practice
that you have been craving? Perhaps a
particular spice or herb you have put
off buying due to the price? (Quality
saffron can really set you back.)
What about that cape you saw and
covet? Or perhaps there is a purchase
you have been putting off, something
as simple as new chime candles.
The internet is the perfect place to
research prices, as there are so many
options. Treat yourself and enhance
your practice. As you surf websites,
cast this spell of intention:

World wide web, offerings abound,
I seek a delight, consider it found.

Emyme

 # June 19
Wednesday

3rd ♑
☽ v/c 7:19 am
☽ → ♒ 10:01 pm

Color of the Day: Yellow
Incense of the Day: Lilac

Altar Cleansing Ritual

Care of sacred space is important.
When we neglect these areas,
they no longer properly reflect our
intent and the care we put into our
magic. First, remove any dust, dirt,
spilled wax, etc. Then use lemon
water to wipe the area and ritually
cleanse it. Simply add fresh lemon
juice to the amount of water you need
and, if possible, allow it to sit in the
sun for an hour. Add a quartz crystal
to the water as well. Use this water to
clean your altar, tools, etc. Visualize
the space being renewed and cleared
of accumulated energy from previous
magical workings.
Chant:

This sacred space is clean and pure,
So the magic will endure.

Ember Grant

June 20
Thursday

3rd ♒

Color of the Day: Crimson
Incense of the Day: Jasmine

Midsummer's Eve

Most witches and Pagans celebrate the summer solstice, but for some, the night before, known as Midsummer's Eve, is just as important. In certain European countries, like Sweden and Finland, it is actually a national holiday. It is said to be a time of magic, mischief, and mystery.

Tonight, as the sun goes down, light a bonfire or sit with a candle in the growing darkness, and embrace the magic of the night. Open yourself up to the elemental powers of nature and, if you like, dance with the fairies under the moonlight. Drink a cup of mead or sparkling water and lift it to the sky, saying:

I am the cusp of the solstice.

I am the mystery on the wind.

I am the magic in the night.

I am power made manifest

On this Midsummer's Eve.

Deborah Blake

June 21
Friday

3rd ♒
☽ v/c 10:02 am
☉ → ♋ 11:54 am

Color of the Day: Purple
Incense of the Day: Rose

Litha – Summer Solstice

Jara Charm Summer Harvest

Celebrate the day by carving your own runic charm to draw the harvest to you. While walking in a park or wildwood today, take a look around for any fallen piece of branch or bark. When you find a tree that calls to you, give it a blessing of milk and/or honey. Say your thanks as you rub a bit of soil from the base of the tree into the woody bark and onto your head as a show of respect. Do your best to identify the type of tree gifting you its earthen wisdom. Eavesdrop…

Using a black-handled crafting knife, carve two right angles, open toward each other, forming the Jara rune (ᚼ). As you work, think about the cycle of the seed and the labor of the harvest. Imagine baskets full of grain and fresh fruits. Envision a pantry and fridge full of produce. When you are done, thank the tree again and bless your charm by rubbing soil into the grooves of your symbol.

Estha McNevin

June 22
Saturday

Notes:

3rd ♒

☽ → ♓ 10:01 am

Color of the Day: Blue
Incense of the Day: Sage

Lavender Dream Spell

This is a time of great abundance, and the herb lavender is in bloom now. Harvest some to make tea to promote sweet dreams, and save some for magical use later on.

Lavender can be used fresh or dried. Known for protection and cleansing, lavender promotes love and has a soothing effect on the nervous system. Taken before bed, lavender tea calms the mind and promotes peaceful dreams.

Place two stems of lavender flowers in a cup, and pour boiling water over them. Steep and serve with honey as desired. Mindfully sip your lavender tea, allowing the sweet aroma and taste to infuse you with a positive, loving energy. Feel your heart chakra opening. As your heart rate and breathing slow, feel yourself relaxing. Feel peaceful and know that sweet dreams await you. Place a sprig of fresh lavender or a drop of lavender oil on your pillow to promote lucid dreaming.

Dallas Jennifer Cobb

June 23
Sunday

3rd ♓

Color of the Day: Orange
Incense of the Day: Hyacinth

Sweetgrass Braid and Blessing

A sweetgrass rite is an evocative way to welcome the spirits of summer. Cultures across North America burn braided aromatic grasses and rushes, not only sweetgrass but also whatever is available locally. Create a sweetgrass braid and then perform this cleansing and blessing.

Cut wild aromatic grasses or sweetgrass (if available in your area) to about forty inches in length. Braid loosely in three strands, like a hair braid.

Stroke the grass braid gently, and whisper your wishes.

Light the braid at dusk. Implore the earth to open the way for you and your family to have an enlightened and abundant summer.

Tamp the flame and travel through your home, clockwise, in the four cardinal directions (east, south, west, and finally north). Spread the delightful vanilla scent and inherent wisdom of the sweetgrass braid along the way.

Focus on encouraging the positive vibrations from the smoke to bless your home. Wet the braid with spring water to put it out. Hang it up to let it dry naturally, until the next usage.

Stephanie Rose Bird

June 24
Monday

3rd ♓
☽ v/c 7:10 pm
☽ → ♈ 10:38 pm

Color of the Day: Gray
Incense of the Day: Rosemary

Write an Inspirational Charm

Elemental fire is associated with inspiration. We "light up" with an idea or "get fired up" to do some task. While inspiration brings rewards in every part of our lives, sometimes we find ourselves running low. Is it time to relight your creative fires?

Appeal to Brigid for inspiration and set yellow, indigo, and violet candles (the colors of the solar plexus, third eye, and crown chakras) on your altar. (If you don't know much about the chakras, go online and learn more.) Leave room on the altar for a clean sheet of paper. Using your favorite pen, write this charm:

Hey diddle dandles,

By the light of these candles—

I'm inspired to write what I know:

_____.

Fill in the last line of the charm. If you can make it rhyme, it will be easier to remember, but rhyme and meter are less important than writing what you truly know.

Barbara Ardinger

June 25
Tuesday

3rd ♈

4th Quarter 5:46 am

Color of the Day: Black
Incense of the Day: Ginger

Spell to Transform Stubbornness

Use this spell to cause stubbornness in yourself or others to lose its grip. On a small piece of paper, write a description of the stubbornness you would like to transform. Rip the paper into small shreds and place in a bowl. Add warm water to the bowl and stir the paper until it starts to disintegrate. Use your fingers to continue mashing the paper until it's reduced to an unrecognizable pulp. Empty the bowl outside and work the pulp down into the dirt. Sprinkle the place with dill or lemongrass. This spell creates a space for new perspectives to enter.

Melanie Marquis

June 26
Wednesday

4th ♈

Color of the Day: White
Incense of the Day: Marjoram

Protective Bug Repellent

Oh no, it's mosquito season! There are many natural ways to ward off these little bloodsuckers besides using chemical-laden commercial repellents. Many herbs that ward off mosquitoes also, coincidentally, possess protective qualities, according to folklore. This herb bundle is a mild mosquito repellent and a protection spell all in one.

Before going out hiking or camping, gather a bundle of some or all of these pest-resistant herbs: citronella leaves, marigold flowers, lemon balm, catnip, lavender, peppermint, rosemary, or basil.

Tie the herb bundle with a white thread. Wipe the fragrant bouquet of herbs all over your skin and clothing so that the herbal scent is all over you. As you do so, visualize white light everywhere that it touches you until you are completely surrounded in protective energy. Guard yourself against mosquitoes and the negative energy of unhappy campers all at once.

Kate Freuler

June 27
Thursday

4ħ ♈︎

☽ v/c 3:51 am

☽ → ♉︎ 9:32 am

Color of the Day: Green
Incense of the Day: Balsam

Communicate with a Salamander

This spell will assist you in contacting a salamander: a fire elemental. Typically, these beings provide energy, help break down boundaries, and sharpen one's will. Invoke them when you need focus.

For this spell you will need some resin incense (I prefer black copal), a charcoal-safe incense burner, and some charcoal.

Light the charcoal. Ground and center. Face the south, or the direction your tradition associates with the fire element. Enter a trance and sprinkle some of the resin on the coal, watching the smoke rise. Call to the salamanders—the conscious beings of fire— to appear in the smoke before you:

> Creatures of the very fire,
>
> Reveal here to me your form.

Look into the smoke with the Witch's eye: your inner sight. Allow the salamanders to reveal themselves to you. Once they have, you may commune with them as you wish.

Storm Faerywolf

 June 28
Friday

4ħ ♉︎

Color of the Day: Coral
Incense of the Day: Mint

A Binding Love Spell

This spell/ritual may be used as part of a wedding, a handfasting, or a commitment ceremony. You could also use it as a private romantic rite. You'll need a field where tall grasses and wildflowers are growing, as well as some jute garden twine and a pair of scissors or a ritual knife.

In the field, the couple should each cut a handful of grasses and twist them together to form a braid. Then they should tie the braided grasses together in the center with the twine. As they both hold the tied grasses, they should say:

> These grasses, which are
> tied and bound,
>
> Unite us forever from toe to crown.
>
> We are bound hand to
> hand, heart to heart.
>
> United, we shall never part.

End by leaving the bundle of grass in the field. It should be allowed to return to the soil from where it came, and again be united with Mother Earth.

James Kambos

June 29
Saturday

4th ♉

☽ v/c 2:38 pm

☽ → ♊ 5:09 pm

Color of the Day: Black
Incense of the Day: Pine

Inspiration Spell

When I'm feeling a bit gray, I cast this spell to fill myself with inspiration and a sense of purpose. In a fire-safe dish, form a square with salt in the center. Then take four yellow candles and dress them with lemon essential oil. Affix them, one each, to the corners of the square. Light the candles and say:

This box I'm in is not for me,

This spell I cast to set me free.

What evades shall come to light;

I break the bounds with all my might.

Now, with your index finger, break the four lines of salt that form the square and say:

Inspiration from on high,

The gift of daemon from the sky.

Muses, spirits, be here now,

A fertile mind for you to plough!

Let the candles burn out and then safely dispose of the remnants.

Devin Hunter

 # June 30
Sunday

4th ♊

Color of the Day: Yellow
Incense of the Day: Eucalyptus

Bewitching Iced Tea

Melissa officinalis, otherwise known as lemon balm, is a calmative herb. It soothes digestion and reduces anxiety, which is great for relieving stress on a hot summer day. Lemon balm is a member of the mint family, so if you plant it, it may try to take over your garden!

To make bewitching iced tea, combine one teaspoon dried lemon balm per cup of water in a Mason jar. Place a lid on the jar and shake. Set the jar outside on a sunny morning and say:

Lemon balm, green and strong,
stir this spell all day long.

Before the sun, high and bright, relieve my thirst when day turns to night.

In the evening, strain the tea and pour into glasses filled with ice. If you like your iced tea sweet, add honey. If you're feeling frisky, add a splash of whiskey to the mixture. Sit back, sip, and enjoy!

Najah Lightfoot

July

In 46 BCE, when Julius Caesar decided to reform the Roman lunar calendar, the names of the months were numbers. He moved the first of the year back to January, and, being the egoist he was, he renamed the fifth month (the month of his birth) for himself: Iulius (Julius, today's July). He also gave it a thirty-first day. (Then he named the next month after his heir, Augustus.)

July (the month of my birth, too) is high summer. In many places, it's the hottest month of the year. It's the month in which everything blooms until the heat of the sun makes flowers—and people—wilt and nearly melt.

What do I remember from my childhood Julys? Rereading my favorite books. Dragging the big old washtub out on the side lawn, filling it with cold water, and splashing all afternoon. Helping my father tend his flowers—roses, columbines, tulips, and hydrangeas. Climbing to the very top of our neighbor's huge weeping willow tree. Chasing fireflies before bedtime and putting them in jars to glitter and wink throughout the night. Sleeping in the screened porch with all the windows open to catch every possible breeze. What are your favorite July memories?

Barbara Ardinger

July 1
Monday

4th ♊
☽ v/c 5:48 pm
☽ → ♋ 9:24 pm

Color of the Day: Ivory
Incense of the Day: Neroli

Canada Day

Firefly Wishes

With the warmer weather come fireflies, also called lightning bugs because of the way they flash on and off. There is something truly magical about standing outside in the dark, warm night and watching these tiny beetles sending secret messages to each other. They might almost be fire elementals, summer heat made manifest.

If you are lucky enough to have fireflies where you live, you can try making a wish on a firefly, sending your own message out into the universe. If not, try watching a video of them online and then visualizing them outside your window. Say:

Firefly, firefly, light up the night.

Take with you my wish and bless it with light.

Deborah Blake

 July 2
Tuesday

4th ♋
New Moon 3:16 pm

Color of the Day: Maroon
Incense of the Day: Ylang-ylang

Solar Eclipse

First Mother's Solar Eclipse Ritual

A new moon solar eclipse strikes wonder and awe. Unfortunately, it is also associated with discord. In Benin and Togo, first mothers Kuiyecoke and Puka Puka worked to end fighting among the villagers. No one listened. To get their attention, they darkened the sun with the moon. The frightened villagers took note and made peace offerings to bring back the light.

Grains have been shared in community since the olden days. Today, make three quick loaves, such as banana bread, tea cake, and cornbread.

Bring the first loaf to a friend with whom you'd like to make peace, at 10:55:13 a.m. EDT, for this is the first moment that the partial eclipse will be experienced.

At 12:01:08 p.m. EDT, bring a loaf to a family member with whom you've had a squabble.

Finally, at 1:22:57 p.m. EDT, the time of maximum eclipse, bring a loaf to a neighbor with whom you've had a misunderstanding. These gestures from the heart will reestablish balance and peace among those concerned.

Stephanie Rose Bird

July 3
Wednesday

1st ♋

☽ v/c 10:25 am

☽ → ♌ 11:19 pm

Color of the Day: Yellow
Incense of the Day: Lilac

Compliment Your Mirror Day

Everyone has heard of enchanted mirrors. Some folks have used mirrors for magic before. Today is Compliment Your Mirror Day, a holiday devoted to self-image and self-love.

This spell calls for a mirror, preferably one you use every morning rather than just for magic. You'll also need some positive affirmations, such as *Your inner beauty shines out for all to see.*

First, turn off the light and imagine how many of your good qualities lie hidden most of the time, unremarked yet always with you. Meditate on what makes you wonderful. Smile as bright as you can. Turn on the light, look in the mirror, and say your affirmations to yourself. The person in the mirror is gorgeous. Take a moment to reflect on what you like about your body. It's okay if you're not perfect—nobody is. Just do your best. Then go on with your day.

Elizabeth Barrette

July 4
Thursday

1st ♌

Color of the Day: White
Incense of the Day: Myrrh

Independence Day

Spell for Freedom

Use this spell to help break free from limitations and other things that bind you. Think about the things in your life that are negatively confining and restricting you from being your whole, best self. Tie a string around your ankle to represent each cage from which you wish to escape. Now take a pair of scissors and call into them all the courageous powers you can muster. If you work with any spirits or deities in your practice, you might consider asking these entities to enter the scissors to impart their strength and power to your spell. When you're ready, cut each string one by one, envisioning yourself free forever from that obstacle. When all the strings have been cut, burn them or cut them into the tiniest pieces possible to help break apart and transform these limitations.

Melanie Marquis

 July 5
Friday

1st ♌

☽ v/c 2:24 am

Color of the Day: Purple
Incense of the Day: Cypress

A Success Spell

July is a potent time for success and prosperity magic of all kinds. For this spell you'll need an orange candle, a pen, a small piece of paper, a few pieces of orange rind, and a square piece of green cloth. First, light the candle and gaze at the flame for a few moments. Concentrate on a specific goal coming true. Then write that goal on the paper. Place the paper and the orange rinds in the center of the cloth. Tie all four corners together to form a bundle. Hold the bundle in your hands above the flame carefully as you say:

> *Success, bless and favor me.*
> *May my goal come to be.*

Snuff out the candle. Hide the bundle. When the wish comes true, retrieve the bundle and burn the paper using the same candle. Discard the ashes. The orange rinds will be dry but can be used for other abundance spells.

James Kambos

July 6
Saturday

1st ♌

☽ → ♍ 12:25 am

Color of the Day: Gray
Incense of the Day: Magnolia

Global human Civil Rights

Ever wished for real equality? Take a moment today, dear reader, to envision total peace in a world where class, education, and advantage do not apply to our human culture. As we evolve in a time of climate change, we are all learning how to share more often. Perhaps the only real thing we can offer as a Western civilization is the democratic and understanding values inherent in civil rights.

In a world of equality, where might all of our egos fit? How will we cope in a future that is increasingly automated? If humanity becomes an obsolete labor force, then what is next for our species, if not equality?

Envision the goals you could fulfill if our natural resources were an equally shared birthright and not an outdated illusion of aristocratic land ownership. Meditate on the words of Martin Luther King Jr., who aptly wrote: "True peace is not merely the absence of tension; it is the presence of justice."

Estha McNevin

NOTES:

July 7
Sunday

1st ♏

☽ v/c 12:50 pm

Color of the Day: Amber
Incense of the Day: Frankincense

Mercury Remembrance Spell

As Mercury goes retrograde, this is a perfect time to go within. We can ride this astrological current, following it backward into a potent or troubling memory, giving us greater insight into how we can better handle problems.

For this spell you will need an orange pillar candle and holder, a nail or implement to carve into the candle wax, and some cinnamon powder.

Ground and center. Using the nail or implement, carve the astrological symbol for Mercury (☿) into the side of the candle. Sprinkle this sign with the cinnamon, working the powder into the carving. Now, with the implement, carve three arrows moving around the Mercury sign, pointing in a counterclockwise circle. Place the candle in the holder. Light the candle, saying:

Moving backward 'cross the sky

Messenger, the winged-shoed god,

Take me as we journey back

Into the memory I seek.

Meditate on your chosen memory, only now with a greater sense of your own power and purpose. How would this play out differently now?

Storm Faerywolf

July 8
Monday

1st ♍

☽ → ♎ 2:07 am

Color of the Day: Silver
Incense of the Day: Narcissus

Accomplishment Spell

M ondays are the beginning of the work week for most of us and are a great day to do a spell to inspire accomplishment. Whether you are self-employed or work for someone else, take a moment to think of three things you would like to get done this week. They could be tasks at work or at home, for your employer or for you. Don't worry, everything doesn't need to be done in one day. Set your sights on having these tasks done by week's end. Plant the seed and let accomplishment grow. Chant:

I know the limits of my physical energy, Goddess be with me.

I know the limits of time and space, Gods be with me.

I know the limits of work and worry, Goddess bless me.

I work steadily without delay or hurry, Gods be with me.

These tasks I will accomplish, Divine ones be with me.

Dallas Jennifer Cobb

July 9
Tuesday

1st ♎

2nd Quarter 6:55 am

☽ v/c 3:36 pm

Color of the Day: Red
Incense of the Day: Ginger

Spread It Around

W hen one door closes, we're fond of saying, *another door opens.* Really? Some days it seems like every door we come to is locked. Nothing's open. If you find yourself feeling poor and unhappy, start with this simple key to open those locked doors: a dime.

We know that magic works better if we spread it around. Collect ten bright, shiny dimes, put them in your right-hand pocket, and take a walk. At each intersection you cross, drop a dime on the sidewalk and say:

For those in need.

Drop dimes near the doors of stores. If someone says, "Did you drop that dime?" shake your head and say, "It's yours."

When you've given away nine dimes, cup the last dime between your hands and say:

For those in need. For me, too, for I'm in need right now.

Keep this dime at your workstation or on your altar.

Barbara Ardinger

July 10
Wednesday

2nd ♎

☽ → ♏ 5:29 am

Color of the Day: Brown
Incense of the Day: Marjoram

Talisman for Defiance

On this day in 1040, legend says that Lady Godiva rode naked on horseback, covered only by her long hair, for tax relief. Despite a lack of solid historical evidence, the legend of Godiva's famous procession remains a symbol of protest. Coventry once hosted an annual reenactment of the ride. Today the Godiva Festival has evolved into a three-day music event.

Largely considered myth, the story is still an inspiration for standing up for something you believe in. To that end, choose a piece of jewelry (or other item) to use as a talisman for your personal protest. It can be a literal symbol of a cause you support or a more private reminder of something you're fighting for. Charge your item using this chant:

For this cause I stand, I fight.
I hold true to what is right.

This symbol helps me stay on track,
keeps me strong under attack.

Ember Grant

July 11
Thursday

2nd ♏

☽ v/c 8:28 pm

Color of the Day: Turquoise
Incense of the Day: Nutmeg

Tiger Lily Courage Spell

The tiger lily, also known as the ditch lily, grows profusely in many parts of the world. These bright orange flowers fearlessly flourish beside highways, in ditches, and in gardens. We can look to this hardy, bold lily when we need the courage and strength of a tiger. If you cannot find a tiger lily, any orange flower can be used instead.

For this spell you will need a small twig to represent yourself, a tiger lily petal, and thirteen inches of orange thread.

Hold the twig in your hand and imagine yourself bravely facing the adverse situation in question like a boldly roaring tiger. Then hold the tiger lily petal up in front of the sun so the rays illuminate it. Declare:

Orange flower, fiery sun,
I'm as courageous as a tiger!

Wrap the stick with the petal, symbolically enveloping you with courage, then bind it with the thread. Leave this charm in a sunny spot or carry it with you until you no longer need it.

Kate Freuler

July 12
Friday

2nd ♏

☽ → ♐ 11:05 am

Color of the Day: Pink
Incense of the Day: Alder

Venus Coin Charm

Happy Friday! Venus rules over love, wealth, and business and also happens to be the ruling planet for this day of the week. Create this charm to harmonize with Venusian energy and use it to increase financial prosperity.

Take thirteen pennies and draw the sigil of Venus (♀) on the heads side of each one with a red paint pen. Once the pennies dry, arrange twelve of them in a circle and place the thirteenth in the center. Draw a pentacle in the air over the center penny, then say:

Hail Venus, Queen of Coin and Heart!

*Be here now, and into
this charm impart*

*Blessings of success and prosperity,
overwhelming abundance and clarity.*

*With your sign this charm is made.
From this world you will not fade.*

Keep the center coin in your purse or wallet to attract prosperity, and spend the other twelve pennies on something that makes you feel successful.

Devin Hunter

July 13
Saturday

2nd ♐

☽ v/c 9:30 pm

Color of the Day: Blue
Incense of the Day: Ivy

Rosemary Home Blessing

Saturday is always a great day for magick for the home. I feel that our homes can use regular blessings, not just when things feel a bit off or when moving. Rosemary is associated with protection, healing, love, and purification. This is a pretty stellar combination of qualities to aim for your home to embody!

Obtain a few sprigs of rosemary and a bowl of clean water, and say a short blessing over the water. Begin at your home's main threshold and move clockwise, dipping the rosemary into the water and using it to lightly sprinkle the water in small droplets throughout your home. Hold your intention to instill the aforementioned qualities into your home with the aid of the plant spirit Rosemary. When finished, thank the spirit, then dry and hang the sprig in your home.

Blake Octavian Blair

July 14
Sunday

2nd ♐

☽ → ♑ 7:05 pm

Color of the Day: Gold
Incense of the Day: Juniper

Magick in the Morning

Arise early and go outside. Face the direction of east. Light a sage bundle or burn herbs on a hot charcoal in a fireproof cauldron.

Watch the smoke rise. Smell the aroma. Be one with the moment. Look toward the light that arises with the dawn. Witness the first call of birds who take flight as day begins.

Know you are a divine being. Know you are blessed. Know the magick is within you.

If you feel called to speak, do so. However, it's not necessary. What's important is your time with nature and the universe. This peaceful time is especially valuable for those who live in cities. Even cities seem to calm down before the sun rises.

When you feel ready to end the ritual, safely extinguish your sage bundle or place the lid on your cauldron. Go about your day, blessed from your magick in the morning.

Najah Lightfoot

 July 15
Monday

2nd ♑

Color of the Day: White
Incense of the Day: Hyssop

A Water Cleansing Spell

With the sun in the water sign of Cancer, this is a good time to use water magic to cleanse yourself of a bad habit or problem. For this spell you'll need a plain white sheet of paper, a pen or a non-permanent marker, and water. You'll also need an old glass or a clean empty jar.

First, write the habit or problem you want to be rid of on the paper. Fill the glass or jar with water. Next, fold the paper and place it in the water. Visualize your problem being diluted and cleansed away by the water. After a few minutes, take the glass jar outside. Now pour the water onto the ground or a compost pile. You may bury the paper or throw it away. In this spell, as your ink begins to fade in the water, your problem begins to weaken.

James Kambos

July 16
Tuesday

2nd ♑

☽ v/c 5:38 pm

Full Moon 5:38 pm

Color of the Day: Black
Incense of the Day: Cedar

Lunar Eclipse

Eclipse in a Bottle

The full moon represents the peak of lunar power, while an eclipse hides and reveals the light. It's a powerful time for revelation and transformation. It's just not always there when you need it.

This spell allows you to store the energy of the eclipse for future use. You will need a silver coin—real silver if you can get it, but silver-colored will do. Hold the coin in your hand and concentrate on making it a vessel for this energy. During the eclipse, lay the coin where the moonlight can reach it. Turn it over several times to expose both sides to all phases of the eclipse. After the eclipse is over, hold the coin in your hand again and imagine sealing it. Now you will be able to use eclipse energy whenever you need it. Ideally, keep the coin in a black bag until then.

Elizabeth Barrette

 July 17
Wednesday

3rd ♑

☽ → ♒ 5:19 am

Color of the Day: Topaz
Incense of the Day: Honeysuckle

Summer Scents

One of the best parts of summer is the way everything is blooming and smells so sweet. Many herbs are at their peak around now, and can be used for magical work both large and small. Rosemary, for instance, is good for mental activities, lemon balm for healing, and basil for prosperity.

Pick an herb or plant that has the qualities you want to work on (if you can't get fresh, essential oils will do), and breathe deep, pulling the magical essence of the plant inside along with its scent. You can say this spell as you enjoy the earthy energy of the plant:

From the earth you have grown,

Your scent so sweet and light.

Lend your power to my magic,

Under summer skies so bright.

Deborah Blake

July 18
Thursday

3rd ♒︎

☽ v/c 11:53 am

Color of the Day: Purple
Incense of the Day: Apricot

The Earth Provides

We are halfway through July and the bounty of the earth is everywhere. At the height of the summer, healthy foods are abundant. What are the fruits and vegetables growing in your particular part of the world? Many farms have "pick your own" sections, from the first to the last crop. Green beans, peas, and cherries are ripe and ready to be picked at this time of year, just to name a few. Perhaps you have planted a garden in your own yard—zucchini and tomatoes flourish in many climates. Create a meal with a special emphasis on nature's plenty. Local farmers' markets often provide recipes specific to their produce: salads and soups, garnishes and side dishes—all created or enhanced by the seasonal gifts from the land. Say:

The four elements come together
and provide nature's gifts,

Blessed by the lady and lord,

For the nourishment of
our body and soul.

Emyme

July 19
Friday

3rd ♒︎

☽ → ♓︎ 5:19 pm

Color of the Day: Rose
Incense of the Day: Orchid

Take Me Away Spell

Use this spell to help manifest the resources and opportunity needed to travel. Collect images of the place you want to go, and assemble these into a collage or booklet. Print out a bunch of your selfie photos, and cut them out so that it's just you in the picture, without any background. Glue your selfies all over the images you've assembled of your ideal travel destination so that you now have a concrete image of yourself in the place you would like to go. Imagine how you will feel when you are there. Put the images somewhere in your home where you'll see them frequently, and place a coin bank somewhere nearby. Try to add some money to the coin bank each day for your travel fund as you imagine how you will feel to actually be there.

Melanie Marquis

July 20
Saturday

3rd ♓

Color of the Day: Indigo
Incense of the Day: Rue

Reverse and Rebalance

While forward motion often proves difficult during a Mercury retrograde, it is a perfect time to revisit and reevaluate positions and tactics so that when the Heavenly Messenger goes direct, we'll be ready. This spell reverses the direction of a bad situation and brings balance.

You will need:

- 2 candles of matching size, one orange, the other blue

- A nail or implement to carve into the candle wax

- Olive oil

- Cinnamon powder

- Dried lavender

Using the nail or implement, carve into each candle the astrological symbol for Mercury (☿), along with a symbol or word that represents your problem. With olive oil, dress the candles, the orange one while focusing on attraction and then the blue one with a focus on banishing. Dust, roll, or sprinkle the orange candle with lavender and the blue one with cinnamon. Place in holders side by side on your altar. Light them both while saying:

Reverse, retrace, revisit, reframe,

Rebalance, regain, remember, rename.

Rekindle, relight, reforge, reshape.

Retry, remark, and resolve.

Let the candles burn down safely. Meditate or do divination to determine how the situation will evolve when Mercury finally goes direct. For when he does, you need to be ready!

Storm Faerywolf

July 21
Sunday

3rd ♓

Color of the Day: Amber
Incense of the Day: Marigold

Eternal Child of Summer

In a parade of laughter and excitement, children have a way of casting a magick of their own when it comes to summer adventures and first experiences. This fun family spell is a great bonding tool that can help keep everyone in the family focused on positive goal-setting for the lazy days of summer.

With your child (or children), other family members, or close friends, venture out to a park or local pond at sunset. Really observe the ecosystem together. Bravely track down and collect an insect for each person. Look for strange and unusual bugs in your area, such as fireflies, and learn about them together using your smartphones or an encyclopedic reference of local fauna. Make a wish as a family and then release each bug. Bring along a picnic and let the warm sunset wash you in the loving glow of the season.

Estha McNevin

July 22
Monday

3rd ♓
☽ v/c 4:34 am
☽ → ♈ 6:02 am
☉ → ♌ 10:50 pm

Color of the Day: Lavender
Incense of the Day: Rosemary

Stretch Your Imagination: Make the Old Myths New Again

Children love to play superhero and change the script. We can do that, too, so let's rewrite some of the old myths. Get out your old Bulfinch (*Bulfinch's Mythology*) and read awhile. Then close your eyes and *voilà!* You're in Mythland. Don your cape. Leap into action.

What if Prometheus entered into a trade agreement with Olympus, Inc.? What if Atreus said, "Whoa, I'm a vegan"? What if Helen said, "Paris, you're swell, but I'm a respectable wife"? What if Midas formed a charitable foundation to sponsor arts and culture…and hired Orpheus? What if Pasiphaë put a collar on that bull and sent it out to pasture?

It's fun to play with the old myths and add modern touches. Movies and games do it all the time. Pagans can, too. Post your remade myths online.

Barbara Ardinger

July 23
Tuesday

3rd ♈

Color of the Day: Scarlet
Incense of the Day: Cinnamon

Grounding Magic

Earthing and grounding are terms used to describe the process of connecting to the earth through bare feet. Earthing has been proven to help ease pain, promote sleep, increase energy, reduce stress, and normalize the body's natural rhythms. Connecting to the earth reduces the stress hormone cortisol and increases natural immunity.

Whether you live in a city, suburb, village, or rural locale, make time to ground yourself today. A book or blanket provides a great disguise. Sit on a park bench and remove your shoes, or lie on a blanket and let your bare feet connect to the earth. Walk barefoot in the park, along a beach, or in your yard. As you connect to the earth, invoke:

Great Mother Earth, heal and help me harmonize me to your vibration that I might be grounded.

Study the effect of grounding on your sense of well-being, and be transformed.

Dallas Jennifer Cobb

 ## July 24
Wednesday

3rd ♈
☽ v/c 10:48 am
☽ → ♉ 5:42 pm
4th Quarter 9:18 pm

Color of the Day: Brown
Incense of the Day: Lavender

Hump Day Spell

Today is Wednesday, known as *hump day*. This term has been popularized by people who work Monday through Friday. Dead in the middle of the week, hump day is what people try to get through as they look forward to the weekend.

Let's try an affirming spell to engage with hump day. Rather than looking backward or forward to the weekend, how about appreciating the magick of Wednesday? After all, this is Odin's Day, and he is the god of poetry and wisdom. It is also the day of the week ruled by Mercury, so it is good for communications. The following spell is designed to ground and center you:

I look neither backward nor forward,

I am here, in the now.

Today is the day I will reach deeply

Into the power of my mind.

I honor wisdom and intentional words.

I look neither forward nor backward,

I am in the here and now.

Stephanie Rose Bird

July 25
Thursday

4th ♉

Color of the Day: Crimson
Incense of the Day: Mulberry

Spell to Banish Debt

To help remove unwanted debt, use this spell. Of course, you must also take practical steps as well. Let this spell help you be mindful of budgeting and other actions you can take.

First, tear up the bills (or copies of the bills) in tiny pieces, visualizing the debt being diminished into tiny, manageable bits. Next, place the pieces in a safe container for burning—a cauldron, fireplace, etc. Light a black taper candle (white can be substituted) and visualize the debt being reduced to mere ashes, easily swept away. Using the candle, light the paper pieces on fire.

Chant:

Debt be gone, no more distress.

It will be handled with finesse.

No more concern and no more woe.

This debt be banished—let it go!

Ember Grant

 ## July 26
Friday

4th ♉

Color of the Day: Purple
Incense of the Day: Yarrow

Charmed Shoe Laces

Quite often we find ourselves at a figurative crossroads in life, caught between two life paths. Symbolically speaking, our feet don't know which fork in the road to take, and we end up going nowhere. That is what this spell is for.

Rosemary is a common multipurpose herb associated with wisdom, memory, and mental clarity, which makes it perfect for decision-making spells and overcoming mental blocks. Make a simple brew of water and rosemary leaves by boiling them together for about three minutes. Once cooled, put the brew in a jar. Now remove the laces from whichever shoes you wear most often. Put them in the brew, tighten the lid, and shake them up. Leave them in direct sunlight for a few hours to give them illuminating solar energy. Leave them to dry, then put them back in your shoes. Pay attention to your intuition during the coming days, and let rosemary, a plant of wisdom, guide you onto the right path.

Kate Freuler

 July 27
Saturday

4ŋ ♉

☽ v/c 12:28 am

☽ → ♊ 2:29 am

Color of the Day: Black

Incense of the Day: Pine

Summer Energetic Cleaning

Many of us do a thorough spring cleaning; however, summer is often a period when hot days lead to a lack of desire to do a deep round of housekeeping. Stagnant energy in the home can be compounded by summer heat and humidity, a really heavy combination. Since Saturday is the day of the week that is ruled by Saturn, today is a great day to do home magick, so let's take advantage of that energetic wave!

First, do what you can to get your home's temperature as comfortable as possible so you can concentrate on your energetic work. Mix up a simple smudge blend of one part crushed white sage, one part lavender buds, and an optional one part sweetgrass. Place safely onto a lit charcoal in a smudge bowl. Waft the smoke through your home, visualizing it as a cool cleansing breeze. Move methodically from room to room visualizing the stagnant energy dissipating and a cooling calm filling your space.

Blake Octavian Blair

 July 28
Sunday

4ŋ ♊

☽ v/c 11:24 am

Color of the Day: Yellow

Incense of the Day: Almond

Solar Power Recharge Spell

With Leo and Sunday both being ruled by the sun, the astrological energies today are perfect for all work related to the sun and its correspondences. Most especially, this is a time for you to work with the sun to replenish your own energy levels.

At dawn, go outside and face the east. Draw a circle with a dot in the center (the symbol for the sun: ☉) in the air and then focus your attention on the dot. Envision this dot capturing the rising light from the sun and then directing it directly into your solar plexus. Breathe deeply and chant this five times:

Sun rising, fill my soul,

Sun rising, make me whole.

Fill what's empty and restore the light.

Bring on the day after night!

Continue to breath deeply, and when you feel you are full, allow the symbol for the sun to fade away. Then disconnect from that energy.

Devin Hunter

July 29
Monday

4th ♊

☽ → ♋ 7:31 am

Color of the Day: Gray
Incense of the Day: Lily

It's Baseball Season!

Who would have thought the simple act of hitting a rock with a stick would develop into America's favorite pastime? Who would think watching nine men run around a diamond shape on green grass could inspire such passion, stories, and myths?

Today, take time to remember the favorite games you played as a kid, and take your inner child to a toy store. You need not buy anything. Just have fun looking at toys, puzzles, games, and stuffed animals. As adults, we sometimes need reminding of how important it is to step away from "adulting" and play a game.

If a toy or game calls out to you, by all means buy it! Thank your inner child for being with you, inspiring you. When you get home, put the toy on your altar to remind you that playtime is good for the soul.

Najah Lightfoot

July 30
Tuesday

4th ♋

☽ v/c 11:32 pm

Color of the Day: White
Incense of the Day: Basil

Becoming the Magician

In the Tarot, the Magician represents mystical influence and knowledge. He stands over an altar laden with symbols of power. Setting up your altar this way is one approach to connecting with the Tarot.

For this spell you'll need your altar, a Tarot deck, symbols of the four suits (typically cups, pentacles, swords, and staves), and a wand. Lay out the suit symbols on your altar, trying to match the image of your Magician card as closely as possible. As an example, you could use a chalice or bowl for cups, an altar plate or pentagram for pentacles, a sword or athame for swords, and a staff or wand for staves.

Take out the four aces and put one in each corner of the altar. Hold your wand over your head. Feel the energy of the Tarot. Visualize it forming a bridge between you and your deck, allowing you to commune with the cards and understand their meanings.

Afterward, return the aces to the deck and your tools to their usual places. It's best to store your Tarot deck on or near your altar.

Elizabeth Barrette

 July 31
Wednesday

4th ♋
☽ → ♌ 9:18 am
New Moon 11:12 pm

Color of the Day: Yellow
Incense of the Day: Bay laurel

A New Moon Purge

Has it been years since you first acquired some of your herbs, powders, and magical ingredients? Your rituals may have become more simplistic, so there may be jars and pots not opened for some time, or you can sense a lack of potency. What to do with all this magically infused yet natural matter? Return it to the source.

Today being Lammas Eve and a new moon makes it an ideal time for this spell. Gather the items you need to dispose of. In a far corner of your property, away from prying eyes, individually pour/shake the items into the ground, returning nature to nature. Chant:

(Name of the ingredient),
you have served me well,

In rituals and spell to spell.

The powers you once held dispersed,

Gently return to the earth.

Emyme

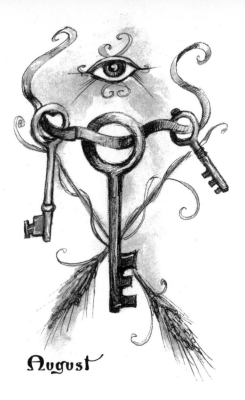

August

Summer is at its height of power when August rolls in, bringing with it the first of the harvest festivals, Lughnasadh (or Lammas), on the first of the month. Lughnasadh is a festival of strength and abundance, a reflection of August itself. Lugh and the Corn God are highly celebrated during this month and are particularly good to work with in spells or rituals for abundance, prosperity, agriculture, marriage, or strength. The Earth Mother in her many forms is ripening and overflowing with abundance. While we often see the first harvest as being associated with corn, there is much more that has been harvested by this point. We must remember not to overlook anything or take anything for granted in our lives, and the harvest is an excellent reminder of that. It is a time to begin focusing on expressing appreciation and giving thanks for all that we have.

The full moon this month is most often called the Corn Moon, but also goes by the Wyrt Moon, Barley Moon, or Harvest Moon. The stones carnelian, fire agate, cat's eye, and jasper will add extra power to your spells and rituals at this time. Use the herbs chamomile, St. John's wort, bay, angelica, fennel, rue, barley, wheat, marigold, or sunflowers in your spells. The colors for August are yellow, gold, and the rich green of the grass and leaves.

Kerri Connor

August 1
Thursday

1st ♌

☽ v/c 4:48 pm

Color of the Day: Turquoise
Incense of the Day: Clove

Lammas

Corn Blessing

Today is Lammas (also called Lughnasadh), the first of the three harvest festival sabbats. Corn is among the popular grains celebrated today, so it's a perfect time to do a blessing of abundance on our homes.

Find a bundle of Indian corn and place it upon your altar. Gather the members of your household around it and hold your hands over the corn, with palms facing down. Say a blessing such as the following while sending your intent into the corn:

Grain of corn, abundantly you grow,

Your blessings aplenty may we sow.

Through the year, may they grow.

Harvests blessings we shall know!

Finish your blessing by anointing the corn with holy water, then hang the bundle in a place of honor, such as above your home's main threshold, the altar, or the hearth.

Blake Octavian Blair

August 2
Friday

1st ♌

☽ → ♍ 9:20 am

Color of the Day: Rose
Incense of the Day: Vanilla

Water Ritual

The goal of this ritual is to explore the water element and get in touch with it personally, renewing your connection for magical or spiritual practice. Find a place where you can hear running water—a stream, a waterfall, or even a fountain. If you don't have access to one of these, you can listen to a recording. The sound of rain would also be appropriate. In addition, use actual water in the ritual, if desired. Consider the metaphysical qualities associated with water, such as cleansing and intuition. In addition, focus on respect for water. Chant:

Water, as you move and flow,

remind us, you're essential—

but with dangerous potential—

the gentle rain, the hurricane.

Keep us mindful, precious water.

Cleanse us, quench us.

Ember Grant

August 3
Saturday

1st ♏

Color of the Day: Blue
Incense of the Day: Sandalwood

Turn Your hotel Room into a Magickal Place

It's the height of summer travel season. While we love to get away, it's comforting to have a bit of home with us when we travel.

Before you take off on your adventure, make yourself a mini-spell travel kit. You'll need your favorite bandana or scarf, a package of salt, and a small bottle of Florida Water.

When you reach your destination, place your scarf or bandana over a lamp shade or table. Instantly you've created atmosphere and added a piece of home to your dwelling.

Pour some salt in your hand, bless it, and add three pinches to a cup of water. Sprinkle the salted water in the corners of your room. Be sure to hit the mirrors, too.

Pour a bit of Florida Water across the inside threshold of your door. Finish by giving thanks for arriving safely at your destination. Know your dwelling is safe and protected.

Najah Lightfoot

August 4
Sunday

1st ♏

☽ v/c 12:27 am
☽ → ♎ 9:30 am

Color of the Day: Orange
Incense of the Day: Hyacinth

In Accordance with Cord and Plug

Have you ever found yourself ensnared in the cables of doom that journey beyond the nether regions from your computer screen or PC tower? Make today the last day of chaos by summoning Mercury, the god of thought, order, science, reason, and electricity to help bring a color-coded system of order to the tangled anarchy of mercurial blasphemy beyond the desktop.

Use colored duct tape to identify internet and router cords. Label each color with a Mercury symbol (☿) and the number of a local or famous highway, such as Route 66, Highway 93, or Rural Road 10. Then make a list of your personal coding system and offer it to the god Mercury as a memento of your devotion to order and reason. Finally, sit before your computer in the quicksilver glow of Mercury's blessing as you feel the ease and precision with which your mind can map your workspace.

Estha McNevin

August 5
Monday

1st ♎

Color of the Day: Lavender
Incense of the Day: Hyssop

Fire Powder

In a fireproof bowl or container, mix together one teaspoon each of powdered cinnamon, powdered cayenne pepper, and ground ginger. These are all spicy, hot herbs associated with the fire element's realm of passion, excitement, and vitality. Charge the powder with these transformative energies by warming it over the flame of a candle or bonfire in the fireproof container. Let the power of the fire permeate the herbs.

To boost the energy of a slow or stagnant situation in your life, shake some of the herb mix onto the earth and command, *Wake up!* Then stomp on it three times, hard. The energy of the herbs, your voice, your intent, and the stomp of your foot will shake up the circumstances and get things moving.

(This powder is hot, so don't get it in your eyes or mouth because it will burn!)

Kate Freuler

 ## August 6
Tuesday

1st ♎

☽ v/c 3:36 am
☽ → ♏ 11:31 am

Color of the Day: Red
Incense of the Day: Bayberry

Enchanted Sounds Fairy Spell

The fae are known for their ability to charm people with beautiful music. They play instruments, sing, and tell stories with mesmerizing skill. You too can gain such skill.

For this spell you will need a bell, preferably of silver or brass but definitely not iron. Invite the fae to join you. Think about how charming their performances are. Concentrate on wanting to improve your music, singing, and/or storytelling skills. Then ring the bell and recite:

Speak and be heard,

Clear as a bird.

Sing and be sweet,

Each note a treat.

Play and make song,

All the night long.

Now ring the bell

And let it tell

All of the fae

To aid your play.

Visualize your skills improving as the enchantment of the fae drifts over you.

This is a spell you can repeat every time you practice. Keep the bell wherever you most often do musical activities.

Elizabeth Barrette

August 7
Wednesday

1st ♏

2nd Quarter 1:31 pm

Color of the Day: White
Incense of the Day: Honeysuckle

Road Trip

In 1909, Alice Huyler Ramsey and three friends became the first women to complete a transcontinental auto trip, taking fifty-nine days to travel from New York City to San Francisco.

This is the time of year when many go on a holiday. How about a visit to Salem, Massachusetts? See the sights at what many consider to be America's "birthplace of witchcraft," a somewhat dubious historical distinction. Best to go before the secular visitors invade the spot in a few months. Or if your tastes run to more literary vacations, go to Tarrytown, New York, and visit the home of Washington Irving, creator of the popular Headless Horseman legend. Every state, every country, and every continent offers vacation sites both magical and educational. Make this a summer vacation to remember. New sights, sounds, tastes, new experiences and expansion of knowledge—travel brings all of that. Let us never tire of these experiences. Go forth and conquer.

Emyme

August 8
Thursday

2nd ♏

☽ v/c 10:58 am

☽ → ♐ 4:35 pm

Color of the Day: Green
Incense of the Day: Carnation

Rue Protection Spell

On a small piece of parchment paper, draw a pentagram. Between each point, draw an arrow directed outward, then dress each of the points with rue essential oil. Fold the paper three times, rotating it clockwise between each fold. Place the folded parchment in a small black pouch, along with five pinches of rue, a pinch of salt, and half of a dried lemon peel. Tie the pouch and then place it in the sun to charge for a few minutes until it is warm to the touch. Then place the pouch in both hands, blow over it three times, and say:

Herb of grace, protector of all,
especially witches, I call upon
your strength and power so that
it may be one with this charm.
Rue, I call upon you to watch over
me and keep me from harm!

Keep the pouch on or near your person for best results.

Devin Hunter

 ## August 9
Friday

2nd ♐

Color of the Day: Pink
Incense of the Day: Violet

Safe Travels

Many people take vacations during this time of year, which often means traveling, whether by car, boat, or plane. If you are going on a trip, try saying this spell before you leave to keep yourself and your loved ones safe. Waft yourself with sage or rosemary incense and visualize yourself and your loved ones traveling surrounded by a glowing white shield of protection. Say:

God and goddess, keep me
safe on my travels.

Watch over me and mine,

And protect me (us) until we have
returned home once more.

Deborah Blake

August 10
Saturday

2nd ♐

☽ v/c 3:50 pm

Color of the Day: Brown
Incense of the Day: Sage

The Sowing (A Modern Opalia, Part 1)

This is a simple multipart spell inspired by the ancient Roman Opalia, a festival devoted to the sowing of crops and the chthonic goddess Opis.

You will need:

- Dried bean seeds (green beans, bush beans, etc.)

- A medium-sized terracotta pot with adequate drainage

- Permanent markers or paints and brushes

- Potting soil

Ground and center. Soak the dried beans in lukewarm water for about an hour. While waiting, design a sigil for your magical goal. Draw or paint this on the pot. Fill with soil and carefully plant the beans about two inches apart and one inch deep. Cover with soil.

Enchant the seeds, saying:

Opis, dark and down below,

Life from darkness rises slow.

Into the light, my future bright,

I will reap what here I sow.

Place the pot in full sun, and water the beans each day while reciting the incantation and focusing on your goal. The final observance of this spell will take place on August 25.

Storm Faerywolf

August 11
Sunday

2nd ♐

☽ → ♑ 12:50 am

Color of the Day: Yellow
Incense of the Day: Eucalyptus

A Zinnia Spell for Strength

In August, zinnias are blooming. I use them in this spell because they symbolize strength and endurance. This spell works well if you're facing any kind of struggle. For this spell you'll need a bouquet of zinnias in any color, or mixed colors. You'll also need some orange fabric, a red candle, and the Strength card from the Tarot.

Cover your altar with the fabric. On the right, place the candle and light it safely. On the left, set the zinnias in a vase. In the center, lay the Strength card. Study the card. It represents quiet inner strength. When ready, say:

I call upon all the power I have within,

To face my struggle,
fighting until I win.

Like the zinnias, I have
the will to endure,

With this spell, my victory is secured.

Snuff out the candle. Leave the card and the zinnias on your altar until the flowers fade.

James Kambos

August 12
Monday

2nd ♑

☽ v/c 6:11 pm

Color of the Day: Ivory
Incense of the Day: Clary sage

Self-Love Spell

Try this spell to help you remember that you are worthy and deserving of love. Challenge yourself to think of at least five qualities that you like about yourself. Choose a small stone or a pinch of herbs to represent each positive trait. Place the stones and herbs in a small drawstring pouch, or bundle them up in a circle of fabric and secure it at the top. As you assemble your bundle or bag, think about each good quality and how you appreciate that quality in other people. Think of how you actually do exhibit each of these desirable qualities. Squeeze the bundle gently as you charge it with loving emotion. Attach the bundle or pouch to a string so that you can wear it close to your heart.

Melanie Marquis

August 13
Tuesday

2nd ♑

☽ → ♒ 11:35 am

Color of the Day: Maroon
Incense of the Day: Cedar

Nemoralia

This is the original day of the Roman celebration of Diana, called *Nemoralia*, or Festival of Torches. There are many roads to approaching Diana's divine nature. She is protector of maidens, grand midwife, friend of the nymph, guardian of oak, lady of the wilds, mistress of the beasts, and goddess of the moon. Hers is a day of equality, appreciation for nature, and making wishes.

To celebrate this day, begin by washing your hair with a fruity-scented shampoo, then dry it however you prefer. Put on a green dress, and dress your hair with flowers.

Using a Sharpie, write your dreams and wishes on colorful ribbons. Gather fresh fruit, toys, or icons of a mother and child, and a stag.

Take the ribbons and items outside to an oak tree. Lay them out at the base of the tree, as an offering. Read aloud the words on your ribbons, then tie the ribbons to the oak. Sit and reflect on your wishes, hopes, and dreams.

Stephanie Rose Bird

August 14
Wednesday

2nd ♒

Color of the Day: Yellow
Incense of the Day: Lilac

Energy from the Fire Within

We've made it to Wednesday, and many of us need some energy to get through this middle day of the week. Let's call a bit of power from without to stoke the fire within.

Gather a piece of carnelian stone and a chime or tealight candle and holder. Light the candle and hold the carnelian stone in front of you in the palm of your left hand. Have the stone positioned between you and the candle. Focus on the light of the candle growing, encompassing you and the carnelian. As its light and fire grows and envelops the carnelian, also see the fire within your own soul growing, energy welling up inside you and the stone. As the energy fields meld together, hold the stone to your heart for a moment. When finished, either snuff out the candle or let it burn down safely and carry the carnelian as a touchstone to the fire that exists within you for strength.

Blake Octavian Blair

August 15
Thursday

2nd ≈

Full Moon 8:29 am

☽ v/c 9:02 pm

☽ → ♓ 11:49 pm

Color of the Day: Crimson
Incense of the Day: Balsam

Celebrate the Fullness of Your Life

Like the year and the moon, our lives move through seasons and phases. August opens with Lammas, traditionally the time of the first harvest. We learned in our Pagan 101 classes that we celebrate the full moon by metaphorically harvesting what we have metaphorically planted. So what's your crop at half past August? How's your life coming along? Consider this: wherever you are today, your life is full today.

Alone or with your coven, cast your customary full-moon circle with white candles and lunar symbols on the altar. State as your intention that you are celebrating the fullness of your life today—the good things like friendships, enough to eat, ongoing employment, etc. If these things have not quite manifested yet, act as if they are here and give thanks. When you describe them, use the present tense. Feel the fullness shining down upon you in the light of the full moon.

Barbara Ardinger

August 16
Friday

3rd ♓

Color of the Day: White
Incense of the Day: Thyme

Elvis has Left the Building

On this day in 1977, the King, Elvis Presley, died.

Many people believe he never really died. He simply went away. His influence on music is legendary; his voice is ethereal and haunting. His hip-swaying, body-shaking movements are memorable and can still excite the heart of a woman who was young and alive when he took the stage in the 1950s.

His home, Graceland, is a sacred place. People from all over the world make pilgrimages to the final resting place of the King.

Today, recall musicians who have influenced your life, for music is the tapestry of our lives and a personal, magickal experience. We all have favorite musicians whose songs have helped us overcome, get through, celebrate, heal, make love, and be inspired. Find one of your favorite songs and give it a listen. Give thanks for musicians and the blessings they bring to all our lives.

Najah Lightfoot

August 17
Saturday

3rd ♓

☽ v/c 6:35 pm

Color of the Day: Gray
Incense of the Day: Rue

Tiny Pleasures Magic

It's said that lots of little things add up to something big. Magic is like that. You don't always have to do big spells and special rituals.

Saturdays are my favorite day to do tiny pleasure magic. While my teenager sleeps in, I slip out to the farmers' market to buy fresh bread, vegetables, fruit, and coffee. I visit with local farmers, friends, and neighbors. I walk to the grocery store for fresh milk and eggs, and the local bakery for croissants or Danishes. Then I amble slowly home, feeling rich. I make a feast. Sitting on the deck, in the sun or under the umbrella, I drink and eat slowly, knowing all the tiny pleasures I enjoy in my community, at home, with my family, and within myself. Life is good.

Today, do your mundane tasks consciously, with enjoyment. Let your tiny pleasures add up to big magic.

Dallas Jennifer Cobb

August 18
Sunday

3rd ♓

☽ → ♈ 12:33 pm

Color of the Day: Gold
Incense of the Day: Frankincense

Burst the Bubble Balloon Spell

Sometimes the status quo just isn't working. Often we feel stuck either emotionally, physically, financially, or spiritually. For moments like this, give yourself a boost by using this spell. All you need is a balloon. As you inflate the balloon, picture the situation you wish to change. Tie the balloon. Chant:

I've had enough, this thing is done,

My patience has been overrun.

It all stops now, time for a break,

I've been asleep—it's time to wake!

Pop the balloon. Repeat as desired. Laugh and enjoy the action of popping the balloon, and let it motivate you to take positive steps in your life to make the changes you desire.

Ember Grant

August 19
Monday

3rd ♈

Color of the Day: Silver
Incense of the Day: Narcissus

The Black hound's Tooth

This spell uses animal medicine to bring protective K-9 spirits to you. Procuring your animal bones from a reputable and humane resource is essential. It is always best to stumble upon any bones you use for magic either while hiking or by looking earnestly for an ethical source—unless, of course, you want your karma dogged by the haunted hounds of Hades. Let's assume not.

Cleanse by washing the bone in sea salt water and then purify it with smudge smoke. Give a blessing of thanks to the spirit of the dog. If you knew the animal or have a kinship with its breed, then offer a prayer to the seed spirit of that species and sing a drumming or keening song to soothe the magic into action. Howling when you are in need or whimpering out for your spiritual pack will help you to feel that this medicine is always with you. Dog magick is about loyalties and devotion. Take the time in your life to commit to those who truly support you, and sink your teeth into the shadow that stalks your sense of peace and repose.

Estha McNevin

August 20
Tuesday

3rd ♈

Color of the Day: Scarlet
Incense of the Day: Geranium

Love as Sweet as honey

By this time in the summer, the bees are happy little campers, dining off the nectar of all the blooming flowers and producing their gift to us: sweet honey. Honey is actually a fabulous natural product. Not only is it delicious on food, but it can also be used for healing. It's a little bit like love that way—sweet and healing and wonderful.

Use some honey (local, if you can find it) to help open yourself to love in all its positive forms. Dip a spoon into the honey and let the sweetness flood your mouth. Then say this spell, visualizing love flying through the universe on its way to you. (Remember that romantic love is only one possibility.)

Love like honey,

Sweet and sunny,

Fly my way

And come to stay.

Deborah Blake

August 21
Wednesday

3rd ♈

☽ v/c 12:06 am

☽ → ♉ 12:37 am

Color of the Day: Brown
Incense of the Day: Lavender

Peace Powder

When calamity strikes or chaos reigns, blend this powder to bring peace and harmony to any area where it is sprinkled. On a clean white surface, create a peace symbol that is roughly nine inches in diameter out of blue cornflower. Fill the inside of the symbol with dried rose petals and then sprinkle this lightly with rose water. Allow to dry, and as it does, chant this three times:

> *Peace to my friends, peace
> to my foes, peace by the blue
> flower, peace by the rose!*

Collect the flower petals, powder them, and then slowly combine them with half a cup of cornstarch or arrowroot powder and say:

> *Floral allies, come to my aid, and with
> all my heart the toll be paid. What
> once was chaos now make calm, flip
> the switch, diffuse the bomb! With
> perfect love this powder be made, to
> bring peace wherever it be laid!*

Devin Hunter

August 22
Thursday

3rd ♉

☽ v/c 5:33 pm

Color of the Day: Turquoise
Incense of the Day: Myrrh

Breakfast Peach Spell

Facing a challenging day? Have an enchanted peach for breakfast! Throughout history in many cultures, peaches have been associated with love, immortality, fertility, and protection—all such lucky, positive things. Even the flesh of a peach is a cheerful hue, not to mention they are delicious and nutritious. When we eat a peach with intent, we can bring into us all of its positive traits.

This spell is for those days when you need some extra personal power, luck, and positive energy to get you started. Using a knife, carefully carve your name into the peach's skin. As you do this, visualize your day filled with joy, luck, and abundance. Eat the peach mindfully, and feel the positive traits entering you and infusing your energy field with sunshine and sweetness. This feeling should stay with you the whole day through, attracting positive people and situations.

Kate Freuler

August 23
Friday

3rd ♉

☉ → ♍ 6:02 am

☽ → ♊ 10:34 am

4th Quarter 10:56 am

Color of the Day: Rose

Incense of the Day: Rose

Life on the Open Sea

You have chosen, or been chosen by, a spirit animal, totem figure, or guide. But have you chosen someone of myth or legend or historical importance with whom you identify? Is there a particular magical type for which you feel an affinity? The fey? Mer-folk? Pirates?

Pirates may not be considered magical, but many identify with these seafaring men and women. What a life: open seas, layered, comfortable clothing, a healthy diet of seafood, plus hats and scarves to cover any bad hair day, which would definitely happen out in that humid, salty air. Of course, this idea is a little silly, but whatever way of life or whatever magical creature calls to you, embrace it. Fashion a token for your altar, such as "gold" coins, real coins, costume or real jewelry, or an eye patch. If you do

sincerely love pirates, then join in with the following ditty:

Yo ho, yo ho,

A pirate's life for me!

Had I my druthers

And not bound to others,

I'd spend my life at sea.

Emyme

August 24
Saturday

4th ♊

Color of the Day: Black
Incense of the Day: Patchouli

Vesuvius Day

On August 24, 79 CE, Mount Vesuvius erupted. Hot ash and pumice buried the Roman cities of Pompeii, Herculaneum, and Stabiae.

This is a good time to honor the element of fire. For this spell you need a red candle, a flat piece of igneous rock (such as pumice), and something to mark the stone. Light the candle and set the rock on your altar. Meditate on how fire can be a source of destruction (as in burning a forest) or creation (as in making new land). Mentally assign one aspect of fire to each side of the stone. Mark them accordingly. Then say:

> The power of fire destroys
>
> All things in time: loves, hates, griefs, joys.
>
> The power of fire creates
>
> All that it takes: griefs, joys, loves, hates.

Imagine sealing those energies in the stone. Later, when you need to change fire's manifestation, turn over the rock.

Elizabeth Barrette

August 25
Sunday

4th ♊

☽ v/c 2:58 am

☽ → ♋ 5:05 pm

Color of the Day: Gold

Incense of the Day: Heliotrope

The Reaping (A Modern Opalia, Part 2)

We began this spell by planting bean seeds on August 10, and have been tending them since then. In this final installment of our modern Opalia, we gather the energy we have generated over the past two weeks and channel it to further bless our personal goal. For this you will need your potted seedling(s), which by now should have sprouted, and a pitcher of water.

Go to your plant. Ground and center. Focus on the sigil and allow this symbol to be emblazoned in your mind. Contemplate the life force of the plant within the pot and how that life force is "fine-tuned" by the presence of the sigil.

Carefully pull up the sprout from the soil. Rinse it with water, saying:

Opis, set upon the throne,

Queen of Lions who wears the crown.

Into this plant: your life and will.

Into my life: my goal fulfilled.

Eat the bean sprouts to embody their power. Now empowered, direct your attention toward your goal and make some tangible, real-world effort toward making it a reality.

Storm Faerywolf

August 26
Monday

4ᵗ℥ ♋

Color of the Day: Ivory
Incense of the Day: Lily

Try Creative Procrastination

Sometimes you just know it's not quite time to make an important decision. That's when you need to do some creative procrastinating. You can sing "Tomorrow" from the Broadway musical *Annie*. Another good song (from *Mack and Mabel*) is "Tap Your Troubles Away." (These are both on YouTube.) You can walk around humming these songs while you're working up to your decision.

When you've procrastinated and tapdanced long enough, find a sage or a crone whose advice you respect. With this person, cast a circle, light a yellow candle (the color of the third chakra: strength of will, sense of purpose), and invoke Thoth or Athena. Lay Tarot card XII, the Hanged Man, on your altar. After listening carefully to divine wisdom and good, human advice and considering what the best decision might be, reverse the Tarot card so he's not just hanging there anymore. Give thanks for inspiration and practical advice... and make that decision.

Barbara Ardinger

August 27
Tuesday

4ᵗ℥ ♋

☽ v/c 4:55 am
☽ → ♌ 7:53 pm

Color of the Day: Gray
Incense of the Day: Ylang-ylang

Energizing Spell

If your home seems to be harboring stagnant energy, try this charm. You'll need a spray bottle full of ice-cold purified water or spring water, plus a small citrine crystal for each room of your home. Walk in a counterclockwise circle around each room as you spritz the ice cold water around the perimeter. Now move your body clockwise around the room with as much motion as is comfortable for you, or simply wave your hands vigorously in the air while envisioning the energy of the room increasing. Place a citrine that has been charged in the sunlight somewhere in the room where it's visible and open to receiving whatever energies the room has to give. Repeat this process for every room in your home. The citrine will remove any lingering negativity while imbuing the space with positive, energizing vibrations. The citrine can be left in each room, or collected into a pouch that is hung up near the home's main entrance.

Melanie Marquis

August 28
Wednesday

4th ♌

☽ v/c **8:07 pm**

Color of the Day: Topaz
Incense of the Day: Marjoram

Protection Stars

These rustic stars act as home protection amulets. You will need:

- 4 black stones or rocks, of any kind (You can find these on the ground; they do not need to be a gemstone or crystal.)
- White or silver paint
- A paintbrush
- 2 white candles and holders

Paint a five-pointed star on each black stone in white or silver. Gather the stones on your altar between the two lit white candles and say:

> *Stones of black*
>
> *And blessing star,*
>
> *Protect [insert name of object, such as "our house" or "our property"]*
>
> *From all harm.*

Place one stone each in the north, south, east, and west corners of your home, a room, or your yard. Stash these amulets around your house, vehicle, or office, or carry one in your wallet or school bag.

Kate Freuler

August 29
Thursday

4th ♌

☽ → ♍ **7:57 pm**

Color of the Day: Purple
Incense of the Day: Apricot

Practice Peace Meditation

August 29th was declared the International Day Against Nuclear Tests by the United Nations General Assembly in December 2009. It commemorates the August 29, 1991, closure of the world's largest nuclear test facility in the former Soviet Republic of Kazakhstan. Today, practice peace with a simple meditation. Sit quietly in a comfortable position, and place your hands in the Dhyana mudra. A mudra is a hand position. Dhyana is one that Buddha is often pictured doing and brings tranquility and inner peace. To form this mudra, place both hands on your lap, right over left, with both palms facing up and thumbs touching. The right hand, representing enlightenment and spirituality, rests atop the left hand, representing illusion. Close your eyes and breathe deeply and slowly. Chant:

> *Om Shanti Om.*

Om is the beginning of the universe, and Shanti is peace. So Om Shanti Om means the universe begins and ends with peace.

Dallas Jennifer Cobb

August 30
Friday

4th ♏

New Moon 6:37 am

Color of the Day: White
Incense of the Day: Mint

Black Moon Meditation and Affirmation

Today you are in for a treat. It is a black moon! Most likely, you can't see it.

We are an ever-industrious and ultra-busy society. The black moon is an opportunity to close off our senses. It's a time to be calm and relieve tension.

Meditation

Go outside and sit down wherever you feel comfortable. Soften your eyes. Leave them partially open and almost closed. Focus on the power and mystery of the seemingly moon-less sky. Focus on your breathing. Count your breaths, making sure to synchronize your inhales with your exhales.

Affirmation

Say:

I soak in the power of black.

I feel safe, nurtured, calm, and light.

Inhale deeply. Say:

I breath in the wisdom of the universe.

Exhale evenly. Say:

I relinquish tension, stress, and busyness.

Open your eyes. Say:

I am of this moment.

Stephanie Rose Bird

August 31
Saturday

1st ♏

☽ v/c 4:46 am

☽ → ♎ 7:08 pm

Color of the Day: Indigo
Incense of the Day: Magnolia

Islamic New Year

A Sardonyx Spell for Clarity

Sardonyx, one of August's gemstones, is a beautiful reddish-brown gem frequently streaked with white. It has many magical properties. It can aid in gaining clarity, finding the truth, and repelling negative magic. This spell for clarity will help you understand any issue.

Perform this spell as you are going to bed. First, write the problem on a small piece of paper and place it on your nightstand. Then hold a sardonyx and silently ask it to help you understand and clarify the situation. Place it on the paper and go to bed. The answer will come to you in a dream, or you may awaken with a hunch, just knowing what to do. Follow your feelings.

When done, place the sardonyx with your magical tools and discard the paper. If you need to purchase a sardonyx, they aren't very expensive and can be found at most gem shops or online.

James Kambos

September

The equinox happens toward the end of this month, heralding the beginning of autumn in the Northern Hemisphere and the start of spring in the Southern Hemisphere. An equinox happens when the sun crosses the celestial equator, an imaginary line in the sky not unlike our Earth's own equator. It's on the equinox that the sun rises due east and sets due west. This is why people often go to famous landmarks to watch the rising or setting of the sun on the equinoxes and solstices. In our ever-changing world, it's nice to know there are at least some constants!

Astrologically, the autumnal equinox is when the sun sign of Libra begins. It's fitting, as this is the time when day and night are of equal length, and Libra is the sign of the scales. The full moon that corresponds with this event is called the Harvest Moon or the Corn Moon. The few days around the equinox and the full moon bring a period in which everything is ripening and full of energy. It all seems to be coming into fullness, preparing either for the coming of winter or the start of the growing season.

Charlie Rainbow Wolf

September 1
Sunday

1st ♎

Color of the Day: Amber
Incense of the Day: Eucalyptus

Golden September

Today is the first day of September. The wheel has turned and autumn is not far behind. Perhaps where you live, trees are beginning to change color or squirrels are starting to bury winter stocks in the ground.

September is a month of change. Take a moment to reflect on the days of summer. How was your summer? Did you take a vacation, go anywhere special, or make any new friends? Was your summer a particularly hard one? Did you experience trials and tribulations? Did life cause you to grow beyond your comfort zone?

However summer manifested for you, take a moment and light an orange candle. Spend a few moments in quiet reflection as the candle safely burns. Feel the magick of autumn and the end of summer just a few weeks away. These are in-between times. Make ready for changes to come. Be one with the first day of September.

Najah Lightfoot

 # September 2
Monday

1st ♎

☽ v/c 4:34 am
☽ → ♏ 7:35 pm

Color of the Day: White
Incense of the Day: Neroli

Labor Day (US) –
Labour Day (Canada)

Career Divination

On this day we celebrate the contributions to society made by all those who perform a trade, skill, or service. Today is all about appreciating the people who keep our civilization and economy moving forward, which also makes it an excellent day to consider matters related to your career and its long-term growth.

Grab a deck of tarot cards. Remove the Ace of Pentacles and place it front of you. Shuffle the deck and then draw eight cards at random. Place the first three cards above the Ace of Pentacles, the next three below it, and the final two on each side of the ace, making a three-by-three square. The cards on top represent your goals, the cards on the bottom represent your challenges, and the cards on either side of the Ace of Pentacles represent how these things are currently manifesting in your life.

Devin Hunter

September 3
Tuesday

1st ♏

Color of the Day: Black
Incense of the Day: Ginger

A Well Full of Pennies and My Two Cents

Leaving pennies for others to find and designate as lucky is a small way of improving your own karma. This fun spell refocuses your attention on serving the needs of others and prevents self-focused attachment to wealth. Even small amounts of money can seem large when in penny form. This spell will take you longer than you might think.

Today, visit your bank and cash $8.88 worth of pennies. Pick a thing that you are eternally grateful for having in life, and give each penny away in the name of that gratitude throughout the day. Take your time and give each penny with a lucky intent, one by one. Be willingly generous today. As you leave each coin, think of the original high value of a penny and be sure that each coin is resting heads up. Do your best to evoke luck and hope in the lives of others and your needs will always be fulfilled if remember to support others when you experience success.

Estha McNevin

September 4
Wednesday

1st ♏

☽ v/c 6:58 am

☽ → ♐ 11:08 pm

Color of the Day: Yellow

Incense of the Day: Lily

Spell honoring Jupiter

The Ludi Romani (Roman Games) was an ancient festival that usually included multiple ceremonies (*ludi*), starting in early September. The ludi of this time are in honor of Jupiter.

For this spell you will need lightning water, which is rainwater gathered during a thunderstorm. The lightning bolt is Jupiter's most feared symbol. It has useful applications in many magickal paths, including Hoodoo. In Hoodoo, lightning water is used as a floor wash to bring fast change and for protection and strength.

Today, make your own Jupiter floor wash. First, sweep your kitchen or living room floor with your magickal besom.

Using a mop or sponge, wet down the floor with lightning water. As you spiritually cleanse the floor, chant:

Son of Saturn,

God of light,

God of peace,

Giver of victory,

Lord of the sky,

Jupiter Optimus Maximus,

I honor you and welcome the power you bring.

Blessed be!

Stephanie Rose Bird

September 5
Thursday

1st ♐

2nd Quarter 11:10 pm

Color of the Day: Crimson
Incense of the Day: Carnation

honoring Pachamama Prayer

Pachamama is the Andean Mama Earth, and is the strong and nurturing force that helps and protects fertility, abundance, women, the feminine, generosity, and ripening crops.

To honor Pachamama you need a small handful of earth, held cupped in both hands. Say:

Pachamama, I honor you.

I pledge to protect and preserve you.

I promise to heal and help you.

I will never abandon you.

Rub earth into each palm and say:

*Pachamama, guide my hands that
I may work in your service.*

Rub earth on your forehead and say:

*Guide my head that I make
good decisions to help you.*

Rub earth on the sole of each foot and say:

*Guide my feet that I may
walk lightly with you.*

Rub earth over your heart and say:

*And guide my heart that I might
always love and serve you.*

Pray to Mama Earth frequently, renewing your pledge to help and protect her.

Dallas Jennifer Cobb

September 6
Friday

2nd ♐

☽ v/c 12:03 pm

Color of the Day: Coral
Incense of the Day: Orchid

Put Your Dream on a Shelf

Sometimes, the world being the way it is, we must postpone a dream. Put it on a shelf until its proper time arrives. Find these ingredients for this spell:

- Black and white candles
- Something to symbolize your dream (such as a picture of the car you can't afford or a map of Paris for the trip you can't take yet)
- A palm-sized cardboard or wooden box with a lid
- A lucky coin (Susan B. Anthony or Sacagawea dollar)
- An agate for grounding
- You might also eat a chicken dinner and save the wishbone. Dry it and paint it sparkly gold.

Cast your circle, light the candles, and invoke Isis and/or Osiris. Fold the picture or map and place it in your box. One by one, place the other objects in the box. Now ask for divine intervention—and patience—as you set your box on a shelf at home or in your workstation until your intuition (or an oracle like the Tarot) tells you it's time to take it down and either burn or bury the contents. Leave it untouched and unopened until your intuition tells you to open or move it.

Barbara Ardinger

 September 7
Saturday

2nd ♐

☽ → ♑ 6:37 am

Color of the Day: Blue
Incense of the Day: Ivy

Balance Stones

The road through life can feel a bit bumpy at times. One source we can tap into to bring balance to ourselves is nature. Being in nature is healing in itself, bringing us back into alignment with our non-human relatives.

This spell requires you to head outdoors for a short hike. On your hike, look for a couple stones. Keep your intuitive ears open for stones that would like to work with you as allies. You'll need two stones, one darker in color than the other. They should be small enough so you can carry them in a small bag but large enough to hold as a touchstone.

When you find your two new stone friends, give them a loving smudge bath by passing them through the cleansing smoke of burning sage or your favorite incense. Then, when you feel you need balance, hold one in each hand and sit quietly, melding with the stones as they create a natural balance and grounding within you.

Blake Octavian Blair

 September 8
Sunday

2nd ♑

Color of the Day: Yellow
Incense of the Day: Hyacinth

Prosperity Tea

Mint has long been associated with wealth and prosperity. Any mint will do for this tea. You can purchase mint tea bags or make your own. Simply prepare it according to package directions, or use your own dried leaves and steep them in hot water for several minutes (depending on the desired taste), then strain. While the infusion is steeping, visualize prosperity filling your life in every way. Imagine that the leaves contain an elixir of wealth, and it seeps into the water, creating a potion for abundance. Chant these words over the liquid as it cools to your desired temperature:

Prosperity will flow to me;

I invite it as I drink this tea.

As you drink, imagine wealth flowing into you. See yourself enjoying the abundance you deserve.

Ember Grant

September 9
Monday

2nd ♑

☽ v/c 4:30 am

☽ → ♒ 5:24 pm

Color of the Day: Gray
Incense of the Day: Hyssop

Fall Cleaning

Unlike most people, I don't do spring cleaning. Instead, I get the urge to clean and cleanse in the fall, before I am stuck in my house all winter. I try to get rid of accumulated clutter, clean and dust all surfaces, and rearrange my altar. This is a good time to clear away any accumulated emotional energy too, and give your home a good going-over with a sage smudge stick. As you clear and clean, say this:

My home is clean and clear

Of dirt and dust, of old troubles and sorrows,

Of anything that no longer works for my benefit.

My home is clean and clear

And ready for the new.

Deborah Blake

September 10
Tuesday

2nd ♒

Color of the Day: Scarlet
Incense of the Day: Cinnamon

Cat's Eye Spell

Aside from being one of the most popular witch's familiars, cats have many special talents. One is seeing in the dark and easily prowling their way through the blackest of nights. We can call upon the power of our feline friends' night vision to grant us clarity during muddled or confusing situations in life. When you are feeling lost in the dark, perform this spell to help you "see" your way. You will need one cat's eye marble and a square of black cloth.

Find a place where you can clearly see the moon, and hold the marble up in front of it, filling the marble with bright, illuminating power. Then wrap it in the black cloth and carry it with you. When you feel confused or lost, remove the marble from the cloth, hold it to your forehead, and let the brightness of the moon flow into your third eye. The path you need to take will become clear.

Kate Freuler

September 11
Wednesday

2nd ♒

☽ v/c 1:22 am

Color of the Day: Brown
Incense of the Day: Bay laurel

We Are One

Let's perform a ritual so that we may remember the tragedy that occurred on this date. Perhaps we can prevent something similar from happening again. First, fill a small bowl with water and drop a pebble into the center. Watch the ripples move outward. Realize that we are that pebble. Everything we do moves away from us, eventually affecting the world. Now say the following:

We are children of the same valleys,
the same forests, the same trees.

We are children of the same
oceans and the same seas.

We are circling beneath the same stars.

The same Creator created us all.

We dance the dance of life beneath
the same moon and sun,

We are different, but we are one.

Today and every day, try to make a difference. Stand up against social injustice, or be a mentor to a child. Maybe if we send out enough ripples, we'll change the world.

James Kambos

♥ September 12
Thursday

2nd ♒

☽ → ♓ 5:52 am

Color of the Day: Green
Incense of the Day: Clove

A Faery Love Charm

Make an offering to the Fae to bring true love. For this charm you will need:

- 6 red roses in a vase
- Green ribbon
- A green candle and holder
- The Lovers card from any Tarot deck
- An apple, sliced on a dish, drizzled with honey and sprinkled with cinnamon
- Some sea salt

Green is the traditional color for the faery folk, so to honor them and ask their favor, we tie the ribbon around the stems of the roses, binding them together, and we offer them apples and honey.

Place the candle in the center of your altar. Behind this place the vase of roses tied with ribbon. Before the candle place the Lovers card, and next to this, the plate with the offering.

Surround this all in a circle of salt. Light the candle and say:

Bring me roses, bring me thorns,

Bring true love into my world.

Let the candle burn down safely. Harvest the rose petals and scatter them in the wind. Your prayer has been made. Now direct your efforts toward making yourself emotionally ready so you can recognize that true love starts within.

Storm Faerywolf

September 13
Friday

2nd ♓

Color of the Day: White
Incense of the Day: Cypress

Full Moon Blessings

I can feel it coming. I can feel the energy of the full moon upon me before I ever see its luminous glow in the night.

Sometimes, if I've planned ahead, I'm ready for a full-blown ritual. Other times, depending upon what life has brought, I may only be able to light a candle. Other times I may only blow a kiss to the moon. All are okay. A full ritual is okay, a kiss is divine, and a candle always lights our way in the darkness.

Tonight, as the moon grows full, let go of what you think you should be doing and simply be with her. Take a nice bath or shower and go outside. Stand beneath the moon and bless yourself, your home, and your loved ones. Let the moon whisper to you and bless you with her magickal light.

Najah Lightfoot

 **September 14**
Saturday

2nd ♓

☽ v/c 12:33 am

Full Moon 12:33 am

☽ → ♈ 6:32 pm

Color of the Day: Black
Incense of the Day: Pine

Harvesting the Moon

Autumn brings the harvest. The full moons of fall used to make it easier to bring in fruits, vegetables, and grains from the field. Now is a good time to celebrate that.

For this esbat, enjoy a feast of fall foods, such as apples, squash, and barley. Ideally, cook your own, but buying it works too. Afterward, step out in the moonlight if you can, or use an image of the full moon over your altar. Focus on lunar energy at its peak. Think of the things you have cultivated in your life this growing season, whether a literal garden or personal projects. Direct the energy of the full moon into those things. Visualize gathering an abundant harvest after all your hard work.

After autumn comes winter, the season of rest. Once you have celebrated the harvest, begin thinking about what you will leave fallow during the cold time.

Elizabeth Barrette

September 15
Sunday

3rd ♈

Color of the Day: Gold
Incense of the Day: Juniper

home Renovation

Is there a place in your home that needs a makeover? Can you finally create your sacred space? Be sure to include magic and feng shui in the transformation: walls painted a color corresponding to the bagua, perhaps new trim to represent completion, new flooring for a firm foundation, or old and new furnishings to honor the past and welcome the future.

When all is done, cleanse the space of the former energy, the vibes of the workers, and the paint/flooring fumes. After that casting, keep a piece of selenite handy. Decorate to enhance the use of the room: calm accents if the room will be slept in, something bright for the kitchen, and books and technology for the home office. Chant:

*A room of my own, a sacred
space; cleansed and cozy, not
an inch will I waste.*

*Romance, family, travel, prosperity;
every corner holds opportunity.*

Emyme

 ## September 16
Monday

3rd ♈

☽ v/c 12:03 pm

Color of the Day: Silver
Incense of the Day: Lily

Casting Acorns

At this point in the year, acorns have begun to fall from the oak trees in some areas. A simple divination can be done with a few collected acorns based on an old traditional method of divination. You'll want to find three or four acorns that look distinguishably different from one another in some way (size, color, markings, etc). Designate one to represent you, one to represent *yes*, one to represent *no*, and optionally one to represent *maybe*.

Hold the acorns in your hands and shake them a little. Think of your question, then blow your breath into your hands and onto the acorns. Then cast them. Read them according to which acorn falls closest to the acorn that represents you. Repeat the process twice more. Look for consistencies between casting rounds to divine the answer. This also works nicely in conjunction with other divination methods.

Blake Octavian Blair

September 17
Tuesday

3rd ♈

☽ → ♉ 6:31 am

Color of the Day: Red
Incense of the Day: Ylang-ylang

September Song

By mid-September it's becoming obvious in most of the US that the seasons are changing. We're moving out of summer's heat and into autumn's welcome cool. Let's celebrate the change of seasons. We can also acknowledge new changes we foresee coming into our lives. Let's celebrate them, too.

Alone or with your coven, state your intention to welcome change. Decorate an autumnal altar with leaves, a few pinches of cinnamon, nutmeg, and vanilla, and a geode in each direction. Lay Tarot card III, the Empress (aka, the Great Goddess), in the center, then draw a personal card. After reading your personal card, sing this beautiful chant by Starhawk:

She changes everything She touches,
and everything She touches changes.

Sing it as a round. Add harmonies. There are long versions (with verses) on YouTube. Learn and sing them. The singing is the working of this spell. You're singing change into manifestation.

Barbara Ardinger

September 18
Wednesday

3rd ♉

Color of the Day: Topaz
Incense of the Day: Marjoram

Harvest Altar

In this season of harvest, consider creating this altar space to help you align with nature's flow. Take a few dried beans or other seeds and place them on your altar one by one as you contemplate what you wish to give to the world today. What are you offering to those around you? It could be kindness, a smile, laughter, or something entirely different. Think about these "seeds" as you go about your daily business. When the day is done, return to the altar with a small notepad and pen. Think about each of the "seeds" you planted and identify what has grown out of each one. Write down a description of your harvest and place it under each seed. This altar will act as a tangible reminder that we do indeed reap what we sow.

Melanie Marquis

September 19
Thursday

3rd ♉

☽ v/c 9:57 am

☽ → ♊ 4:58 pm

Color of the Day: Turquoise
Incense of the Day: Jasmine

BFFs for the Foreseeable Future

As much as we may be innocently prone to bond with new people prematurely, learning to take trust and friendship in stages is vital to finding lifelong confidants.

Cast this spell with any new friend whom you hope will stick around. Procure one spool of yellow ribbon and a dozen yellow roses with baby's breath. Bundle the flowers into two bouquets for each other. As you bind the roses with the yellow ribbon, speak your feelings of rapport and express hope for deeper levels of trust in the future.

During this "getting to know you" phase, dry the flowers upside down as a symbol of your new acquaintance. Take care: once a tussie-mussie of fidelity is exchanged, any sign of rot or damage on the bouquet is believed to be a curse to the alliance, so be sure to be mindful of the bouquet's drying health!

Estha McNevin

September 20
Friday

3rd ♊

Color of the Day: Pink
Incense of the Day: Violet

Dies Veneris Ritual

Dies Veneris means "day of Venus," which is Friday. Venus is the Roman goddess of love, beauty, and victory. She's a self-possessed and sensual goddess. Today is a good day to do a ritual in her honor.

Begin by taking off your clothes. Light a pink floral-scented candle in a holder.

Into a cup of coarse sea salt, crumble the petals of a single pink or red rose. Say:

In honor of Venus.

Sprinkle the sea salt mixture in the tub. Draw a hot bath and swirl the mixture to dissolve.

Take a clamshell-shaped soap and natural sponge into the tub. Recite:

I conjure Venus.

Rub soap on the sponge and wet it to create a lather. Cleanse your body. Say:

May I learn from the love magick, beauty and acceptance of self. I ask these things of you on your day. Blessings to Venus!

Bathe in the light and warmth of the candle. See what messages Venus brings forth for you.

Get out of the tub and dry off. Put on a robe and record any visions or messages you receive. Extinguish the candle.

Stephanie Rose Bird

September 21
Saturday

3rd ♊

☽ v/c 10:41 pm

4th Quarter 10:41 pm

Color of the Day: Indigo
Incense of the Day: Sandalwood

UN International Day of Peace

Candle Spell for Peace

Today, in honor of the UN International Day of Peace, perform this ritual. Carve a peace sign into a light blue or white votive candle, and surround it with clear quartz points. Light the candle and visualize comfort, love, acceptance, and kindness spreading across the world like a soft blanket. Imagine your energy, represented by the candle, being amplified by the crystals, joining with the peaceful intentions and actions of others, united in a common goal. Chant:

Let love and peace fill hearts and minds,
never ceasing 'til it finds
its way to all, with fear dispelled—
all hate and violence to be quelled.

Let the candle burn out safely. In addition, take some action today: do something kind for someone, display symbols of peace, attend an event, make a donation, etc.

Ember Grant

September 22
Sunday

4th ♊

☽ → ♋ 12:50 am

Color of the Day: Orange
Incense of the Day: Frankincense

Equinox Preparation Bath

Tomorrow is the fall equinox, and the tides of seasonal energies will shift once again, ushering in change and a series of new cycles. Tonight, take this cleansing bath (or dissolve this mixture in water and use it like body wash in the shower) to prepare for this shift and open the way for those new cycles.

Combine one cup sea salt with nine drops of hyssop essential oil, five pinches of both dried lavender and dried sage, and three pinches of dried lemongrass. Mix well, and as you do so, recite the Charge of the Goddess. Then seal the blessing by saying:

What is within shall now be free, for what I have sought I have found!

Let there be ending and completion, renewal and new beginnings.

May the mysteries continue and the magic flow! Blessed be.

Devin Hunter

September 23
Monday

4th ♋

☉ → ♎ 3:50 am

☽ v/c 6:05 pm

Color of the Day: Ivory
Incense of the Day: Narcissus

Mabon – Fall Equinox

Gratitude Ritual

Happy fall equinox! Today marks the second harvest, a time of thanksgiving and celebration. Day and night are exactly equal in length on this date, and after today, the moon will officially get more sky-time than the sun until spring.

Here is a simple ceremony to be performed on the fall equinox to give thanks for all that we have harvested this year, to share a toast with the earth, and to welcome the season of darkness.

Gather thirteen nuts or berries and a glass of apple cider or wine. Go outside at dusk and dig a shallow hole in the earth. One at a time, hold a nut or berry in your hand, state something you are thankful for, and place it in the ground. Do this for all your nuts or berries, then bury them. Pour some of your beverage onto the spot and then take a sip of it. Next, hold your glass up to the west and say cheers to the coming darkness. Watch night fall as you enjoy your drink.

Kate Freuler

September 24
Tuesday

4th ♋

☽ → ♌ 5:19 am

Color of the Day: Gray
Incense of the Day: Bayberry

Spinning into Wisdom

Autumn is a time of balance, when the dark and cold are slowly growing stronger as the heat and light recede. The seasons have a dynamic balance, always changing yet never out of balance. A top, like the seasons, finds its balance through spinning.

For this divination spell, you need a big sheet of paper and a spinning top. Think of a question. Meditate about its importance. Toward the center of the paper, write down all the possible steps along the way to your question's resolution. Toward the edge, write the different possible outcomes or answers. Draw lines between the entries to define areas.

Put the paper on a table. Give the top a spin and release it in the center. Note the path that it takes: these are the most likely things you'll actually encounter along the way. The place where the top falls over or leaves the paper indicates the probable resolution to your question.

Elizabeth Barrette

September 25
Wednesday

4th ♌

☽ v/c 12:14 pm

Color of the Day: White
Incense of the Day: Lavender

Take the Day Off

No matter what type of day you had—stressful or easy—before you get settled into your home for the night, take the day off. This spell works best if you have a small foyer at the main entrance to your home; however, it can be modified for any dwelling. You will need a bowl made from natural material, about the size of a cereal bowl or slightly larger, filled with water. Stand before the bowl and sweep your hands down your body, not quite touching, from head to waist, and "throw" the day's energy into the water. Then sweep from waist to feet. Sweep down each arm, all the while putting forth the intention of cleansing the day from your body and mind. Place everything in the water. Then toss the water in the toilet, flushing away the world's "dust." Say:

Take the day off,

Leave it behind.

Cleanse the body,

Calm the mind.

Emyme

September 26
Thursday

4th ♌
☽ → ♍ 6:37 am

Color of the Day: Purple
Incense of the Day: Balsam

Wish Upon an Apple Spell

Apples are a most magical fruit. Perform this spell in September, when apples are at their peak.

Go where apples grow, and select
a fruit still upon the tree.

The color of crimson red it should be.

While you hold your wish
in your thoughts,

Wash it clean of all specks and spots.

Cut your magical fruit in half,
and eat one half before bed.

On paper, write your
wish in ink of red.

Set your wish and other apple
half upon your windowsill.

Before retiring, into the
apple project your will.

Upon arising the next morn,
while you're all alone,

Bury the remaining half and
your wish near your home.

Your wish must be kept secret,
now and forever more.

Tell no one, even after
the wish is yours.

James Kambos

September 27
Friday

4th ♏

☽ v/c 11:58 pm

Color of the Day: Rose
Incense of the Day: Thyme

Putting Away the harvest

We are fully into the fall season now, between the second and third harvest festivals (Mabon and Samhain). Those of us who grow gardens are putting them to bed for the winter. It can be bittersweet to pull up the final harvest and mark the end of the growing season, but it is also a relief to slow down and rest for a bit. This is true for people as well. The end of the growing season reminds us that all things have their time, and the cycle of growth and death means that resting is a part of life. So give yourself permission to put down your tools, whatever they are, and slow down a bit as you move into the darker days. Light a black candle, take a deep breath, and say:

The harvest is over. I allow myself to rest and relax. Ahhhh.

Deborah Blake

September 28
Saturday

4th ♏

☽ → ♎ 6:03 am

New Moon 2:26 pm

Color of the Day: Blue
Incense of the Day: Magnolia

Gypsy Luck, by Hades or High Water

Mother Nature continues to give us evidence of the importance of water in all its emotionally catastrophic and creative capacities. It can sometimes be from this place of spiritual no-thing-ness that our deepest desires and karma emerge. Our True Will is a divine destiny, a kind of egg that we have to crack.

Living out our deepest losses and still choosing to care and share is a matter of consciousness and nonattachment. In your darkest hour, be encouraging toward yourself and others. You can calmly and deliberately choose to blossom because of adversity with a bit of Gypsy luck on your side.

In a saucepan, place the following:

- 1 broken egg, shell and all
- 1 leafy sprig tulsi (holy basil)
- 3 kernels of allspice
- 1 cinnamon stick
- 1 cup of honey
- 1 bottle of horrible red wine

Warm over medium heat until the egg is completely cooked. Strain into the original wine bottle and consume a glass daily for luck, nutrition, regained vigor, and mood improvement.

Estha McNevin

September 29

Sunday

NOTES:

1st ♎

☽ v/c 10:06 pm

Color of the Day: Yellow
Incense of the Day: Almond

Friend-Finding Spell

If you want to attract more positive, supportive people into your life, try this spell. You'll need a candle in your favorite color, a heat-resistant dish, a piece of your hair or a drop of your saliva, and a small pinch of rosemary or lavender. Keep your supplies at the ready, as you will need to work quickly to cast this magick. Light the candle and drip some of the wax onto the heat-resistant dish. Think of your good qualities as a friend as you add your hair or saliva to the wax. Sprinkle on the herbs, then mold the wax into a heart shape as you envision yourself as the life of the party, surrounded by a group of laughing, loving, loyal friends. Carry the heart with you to attract good company.

Melanie Marquis

September 30
Monday

1st ♎

☽ → ♏ 5:42 am

Color of the Day: Lavender
Incense of the Day: Clary sage

Rosh hashanah (begins at sundown on September 29)

Turning Over a New Leaf

This is a spell to bless the resolution of a new habit or practice. You will need:

- A green candle in a holder
- A nail or implement to carve the candle
- A bay leaf
- An ink pen suitable for writing on the bay leaf
- 4 pieces of quartz crystal
- A cauldron or fire-safe ash pot

Create a sigil to represent your resolution and carve it into the candle using the nail or implement. Carefully draw this sigil on the bay leaf, then place the leaf face down in the center of your altar, with the candle just behind it. Then place the crystals (representing the four directions) on the corners of the altar.

Reach out and take hold of the bay leaf. Flip it over in a motion toward yourself, over and over, seven times, while saying:

This new leaf I turn and turn.

My new life begins right now.

Carefully burn the leaf in the flame of the candle and toss it into the cauldron or pot. Dispose of the remnants in any way you desire. Allow the candle to burn down safely. As your new habits are challenged, remember the sensation of turning the leaf in your hands as a mental charm to keep you on your new path.

Storm Faerywolf

October

Days that turn on a breath into rapidly waning light. Wispy, high dark clouds in an orange and turquoise sky. Bright orange pumpkins carved into beautiful art and lit from inside. The eerie music of screeching cats. These fond images of October burn at a Witch's heart, calling to her even across the seasons where she's busy setting up her tent for festival. By the time October finally arrives, Witches and other magic users have already had discussions about costumes and parties, rituals and celebrations, and we look forward with happiness to the whole month of both poignantly somber and brightly playful activities.

In Celtic Europe, our ancestors acknowledged October as the last month of the summer season, with winter officially beginning on Samhain. They carved slits in squashes to keep light in the fields so they could finish their day's work, and when the custom came to America, it eventually evolved into the tradition of carving jack-o'-lanterns. American Witches often use magical symbols to carve their pumpkins, creating beacons for their Beloved Dead. In the spirit of the turn of energies at this time, we give candy to children to ensure that they, our future, will remember the sweetness inside and be good leaders when their turn comes. May we all be so blessed.

Thuri Calafia

October 1
Tuesday

1st ♏

Color of the Day: Black
Incense of the Day: Geranium

Forget a Lover Spell

This spell will help you get over an old lover. You'll need a black candle, a sheet of gray construction paper, and a sprig of bittersweet (it helps you forget). You'll also need two crayons, one white and one black.

Place the candle in the center of your altar and light it. On the paper, using the white crayon, write your name and your former partner's name. Lay the paper in front of you—you'll use the black crayon later. Hold the bittersweet. Then repeat these words three times:

A love that was strong is now gone.

Each time you repeat this charm, speak more softly. Lay the bittersweet aside. Now with the black crayon, make an X across the names. Let the candle burn a while, then safely blow it out with force. When the candle is cool, wrap it along with the bittersweet in the gray paper and throw it in the trash.

James Kambos

October 2
Wednesday

1st ♏

☽ v/c 5:46 am
☽ → ♐ 7:44 am

Color of the Day: Brown
Incense of the Day: Bay laurel

Archangel Michael Blessing

Archangel Michael is quite a specimen: buff, tan, and handsome, yet so much more. He is the archangel of protection. His brawny muscles are there to ease your fears. His color is a soothing purple.

Go out today and find or purchase a purple feather. Once you have the perfect feather, sit with it outside, holding it to your heart.

Call to him:

*Michael, I call to you
with an open heart.*

I ask you to protect me.

*With your mighty sword,
shield me from all harm.*

Hold the feather in the palm of your dominant hand and say:

Bathe me in your warming energy.

*Light as a feather, through you,
I am healed, inside and out.*

Do an inner scan of your body, mind, and spirit. Check for warmth—flushed cheeks, tingling hands or feet, spreading warmth, or a fresh smile on your face. These are signs that he has listened. Go forward. Be bold and take chances.

Stephanie Rose Bird

 October 3
Thursday

1st ♐

Color of the Day: Green
Incense of the Day: Carnation

Petitioning the Dead Spell

If you would like to ask for help or information from someone who has passed away, you can try this spell to help open a line of communication between yourself and the dead. Write a letter to the soul you wish to contact, including the full name of the person and all the details of your request. If possible, place the letter directly on the person's grave. If this isn't an option, you can tuck the letter among the roots of the oldest, largest tree you can find, or bury it in a cemetery. Pay attention to signs, symbols, dreams, visions, and any other unusual occurrences that you experience over the course of the next several days. If you're seeking a more detailed or clear-cut message, a talking board (aka ouija), pendulum, automatic writing, or other tool of spirit communication may also be used.

Melanie Marquis

October 4
Friday

1st ♐

☽ v/c 3:34 am

☽ → ♑ 1:43 pm

Color of the Day: Pink

Incense of the Day: Mint

Spirit Animal Wax Talisman

Today is World Animal Day, and all over the globe people are celebrating and bringing awareness to animals and causes related to animal rights. In honor of this, and to tap into the potent energy of animal-human partnership, create this talisman to help you grow in power and resonance with your spirit animal.

Etch a depiction of your spirit animal onto a small wax disc. (These can easily be made by melting wax and pouring a shallow amount into muffin tins to harden.) Connect to your spirit animal and ask it to join you and to share its medicine by placing a piece of its energy into this wax disc. When you feel that this has been done, seal the energy by painting the etching gold. Save this talisman and use it to empower other objects with similar energy.

Devin Hunter

October 5
Saturday

1st ♑

2nd Quarter 12:47 pm

Color of the Day: Gray

Incense of the Day: Rue

Anti-Stress Mud Mask

There is nothing like a good mud mask to help evoke the grounding and curative powers of Mother Earth. If the transitory demands of the season have you feeling stressed, take a minute today to ground down. In 33 minutes, this mask will have you looking years younger and feeling noticeably more secure.

In a large glass bowl, combine the following ingredients:

- 2 cups bentonite clay
- 3 tablespoons turmeric
- 1 teaspoon asafoetida (hing)
- 1 teaspoon cinnamon
- 1 teaspoon Norwegian fish oil extract
- ½ teaspoon angelica powder
- 8 drops organic tea tree oil
- 1 cup of brewed Matcha green tea

Mix the mask thoroughly until a smooth paste forms. Apply while warm and relax into a chair or hot

bathtub. Offer the following prayer
three times:

> Demeter decree, my discreet
> and determinant adaptivity!

Rinse clean using only warm water,
and moisturize with a mild face cream
rich in vitamin E for best results.

Estha McNevin

October 6
Sunday

2nd ♑

☽ v/c 7:25 pm

☽ → ♒ 11:42 pm

Color of the Day: Gold
Incense of the Day: Heliotrope

Communicate with an Undine

This spell will assist you in
contacting an undine: a water
elemental. Typically, these beings
provide emotional healing, the ability
to delve deep into our subconscious,
and a general feeling of emotional
renewal. Invoke them when you feel
depressed or lacking in passion.

For this spell you will need a blue
candle in a holder and a glass of water.

Face the west, or the direction
your tradition associates with the
water element. Ground and center.
Place the candle on your altar, with
the glass of water in front of it.
Enter a trance and gaze through the
water so that you can see the light
of the candle through it. Call to the
undines—the conscious beings of
water—to appear before you:

> Creatures of the flowing water,
>
> Reveal here to me your form.

Look into the water with the Witch's
eye: your inner sight. Allow the
undines to reveal themselves to you.
Once they have, you may commune
with them as you wish.

Storm Faerywolf

October 7
Monday

2nd ♒

Color of the Day: Silver
Incense of the Day: Rosemary

Bringing the Autumn Rains

In a temperate climate, spring and fall are typically the rainy times. Summer tends to be dry, while winter brings snow. That is no longer as reliable as it used to be. So here's a spell to bring the autumn rains.

To cast this spell, you'll need some fresh colorful autumn leaves and some dry brown ones, plus a bowl of water. It's easier to do this outdoors, but you can bring some leaves indoors if necessary. Dip a handful of fresh leaves into the bowl and sprinkle water in all four directions, then above and below. Say:

Hear me, autumn rains,
wherever you may be.

Dip the fresh leaves again and sprinkle water onto the dry leaves. Listen to the familiar sound it makes. Say:

Come hither, autumn rains,
wherever you may be.

Preferably, dispose of the leaves outdoors and pour the water over them.

Elizabeth Barrette

October 8
Tuesday

2nd ♒

☽ v/c 2:27 pm

Color of the Day: Red
Incense of the Day: Cedar

Wish Bracelet Spell

Get a piece of thread that is about ten inches long. Hold it in the smoke of burning incense while thinking of your wish, then wrap it around your wrist or ankle. As you make a bow, say your wish aloud. Now your wish is inside the bow, empowered by air, the element of communication and dream fulfillment. Choose the color of thread according to your wish:

Green—money

Red—love

Pink—friendship

Orange—success

Yellow—happiness

Blue—peace

Purple—psychic power

Black—protection

White—all-purpose

Leave the bracelet alone and do not take it off for any reason. Forget about it if you can, and let it fall off of its own accord. This can take hours or days or even weeks. When it does, your wish will start to manifest.

Kate Freuler

October 9
Wednesday

2nd ♒

☽ → ♓ 12:05 pm

Color of the Day: Yellow
Incense of the Day: Lilac

> Yom Kippur (begins at
> sundown on October 8)

Atonement Spell

Today is Yom Kippur, the Day of Atonement in Hebrew culture, when Jews seek to purify their souls. Atonement (at-one-ment) means to be "at one" with ourselves. In twelve-step programs like AA and NA, the fourth step reads: "We made a searching and fearless moral inventory of ourselves."

Today, write your own inventory. List your liabilities and assets. Guilt, shame, remorse, self-pity, resentment, betrayal, fear, and denial have a place on this list, as do honesty, open-mindedness, willingness, courage, faith, kindness, generosity, and gratitude.

Look at your list and say:

I see all that I am.

Fold the list in half and say:

*At-one-ment. I make peace
with all that I am.*

Fold the list again and say:

*Atonement. I purify my soul. I see my
self, light and dark. I know who I am.*

*Going forward I am guided.
I am all that I am.*

Place the list on your altar. Be at one with yourself. Grow. Change. Atone.

> Dallas Jennifer Cobb

October 10
Thursday

2nd ♓

Color of the Day: White
Incense of the Day: Clove

Make a Talisman

Go out among the autumn trees and look for twigs lying on the ground. Gather several that are about six inches long and preferably forked. If you can't find twigs, you can use six-inch pieces of doweling or popsicle sticks or whatever else you think of. You can make these twigs into talismans for yourself and winter holiday gifts for your friends. (If you live where there are, alas, no trees that drop twigs, you can use Popsicle sticks or pieces of dowel rods.)

Gather these supplies out of your art and magic cabinet:

- Beads
- Magical stones and herbs
- Mini squeeze bottles of sparkly paint
- Embroidery floss and/or ribbons
- Tiny feathers
- Other decorative items that call to you

First, speak aloud your intention for this talisman's magic. Then paint a face on the twig. Depending on what the magic is for, tie stones, beads, feathers, and anything else that calls to you on the twig. Make it beautiful and fancy. (If anybody asks, you're Making Art.)

Cast your circle and state your intention. Afterward, set the talisman in its best place or hang it on the wall.

Barbara Ardinger

·October 11

Friday

2nd ♓

☽ v/c 5:55 am

Color of the Day: Purple
Incense of the Day: Violet

In Service to Equality

Today is the birth date of Eleanor Roosevelt, America's longest-serving first lady. Eleanor Roosevelt was a strong civil rights supporter and served as a strong voice in favor of equal pay and benefits to be extended to all races in an administration with official positions that were mostly to the contrary. Even in our current times it is plain to see that there are many civil rights battles that are still ongoing. Let us remember Eleanor and continue to strive for the equality of all people as we examine our relationships to others in society. Light a candle and recite:

> Candle burning bright,
>
> Passion for equality may it ignite.
>
> Illuminate the ways for me,
>
> That I may be of service
> to those around me.

Contemplate how you can make a positive contribution to civil rights movements. How can you help lift others and create positive change? Journal your thoughts.

Blake Octavian Blair

·October 12

Saturday

2nd ♓

☽ → ♈ 12:46 am

Color of the Day: Black
Incense of the Day: Sandalwood

Fire Spell for Strength

This ritual celebrates the characteristics of the fire element, helping you draw those qualities, as needed, into your life. Fire governs the realms of change and transformation, courage, energy, and passion. It can also be used for protection and purification and for banishing negativity.

Focus on your needs, including gaining strength, as you meditate on the element of fire. Light candles or incense or make a fire in a fireplace or patio fire pit. Contemplate the qualities of fire and the ways in which it's essential for our lives. As with all the elements, fire can be destructive, so we must always treat it with respect. Chant:

> Fire, in my darkest hour,
> spark my strength and untapped power.
>
> Bring me what I need to thrive,
> to persevere and to survive.

Ember Grant

October 13
Sunday

2nd ♈

Full Moon 5:08 pm

☽ v/c 5:59 pm

Color of the Day: Yellow
Incense of the Day: Marigold

Spell for Courage

Use this spell to increase your sense of confidence and courage so that you can face any challenges that arise with greater strength and bravery. Stand outside under the light of the full moon and sprinkle around your feet a circle of powdered cinnamon. Strike your most courageous pose and imagine that you are an all-powerful superhero with supernatural abilities as you invite the moonlight to pour into your body. Howl at the moon if it seems fitting, imagining yourself as a wild and untamable beast, fierce and full of vigor. When you feel as if you've got a good fake courage going on, imagine lions, crocodiles, or other symbols of danger lurking just beyond the perimeter of cinnamon that surrounds you. Take a step or leap out of the circle of cinnamon as you say *boo!* at the imaginary dangers.

Melanie Marquis

 October 14
Monday

3rd ♈

☽ → ♉ 12:24 pm

Color of the Day: Ivory
Incense of the Day: Narcissus

Columbus Day ~
Indigenous Peoples' Day ~
Thanksgiving Day (Canada) ~
Sukkot begins (at sundown
on October 13)

Pumpkin Seed Prosperity

Here is a fun magical exercise to do as you are carving your Halloween pumpkin (into something witchy, no doubt). Seeds are symbols of abundance and prosperity, so as you scoop all that lovely gunk out of your Jack o' lantern, use the seeds to do some simple prosperity magic. With each seed (or handful of seeds, depending on the size of your pumpkin), state aloud your wishes for prosperity, in all its forms. Then, if you want to, roast the seeds and eat them, taking all that prosperity energy back inside. As you eat each seed, say or think:

*With this seed, I have the prosperity
I desire in the best way possible.*

Deborah Blake

October 15
Tuesday

3rd ♉

Color of the Day: Maroon
Incense of the Day: Basil

Recharge Your Batteries

It's autumn. Days are shortening. Nights are lengthening. The colors of fall are at their peak. As the wheel turns and the seasons wind down, take a moment to let go and enjoy the golden days of autumn.

Find a grassy spot where you can lie down. Resist the temptation to rest on a blanket. Simply plop yourself down on Mother Earth and look up at the sky. Feel the support she gives you. Run your fingers through the grass. Enjoy the sensation, for as sure as grass is green, we know winter will be here soon in climates where the seasons change. Our glittering green grass will be a nostalgic memory.

As you lie on your back, gaze at the sky. Look at the clouds and marvel at their wispy, willowy shapes. Enjoy this moment brought to you by the blue skies of autumn.

Najah Lightfoot

October 16
Wednesday

3rd ♉
☽ v/c 4:37 am
☽ → ♊ 10:30 pm

Color of the Day: Topaz
Incense of the Day: Lavender

Boss's Day Hoodoo Spell

In Hoodoo, there are many spells (also referred to as *tricks* or *jobs*) related to career issues. One of the herbs (a tuber) used for this area of magick is called Little John to Chew, or simply Little John. The botanical name is *Alpinia galanga*, and it is also called greater galangal.

Little John resembles ginger in taste, medicinal qualities, and structure. It calms the stomach, deodorizes the mouth and body, soothes frazzled nerves, and, most importantly here, appeals to your boss, for today is Boss's Day.

For this spell, obtain a fresh Little John to Chew root. Shred some of it into small pieces (about a teaspoon). When you approach your boss's office or your would-be boss's location, begin chewing the prepared root. State your complaint, desires, or wishes to the boss while chewing Little John. Once outside, spit it out on the property. Your wishes will be heard and respected by the boss. Happy Boss's Day!

Stephanie Rose Bird

October 17
Thursday

3rd ♊

Color of the Day: Turquoise
Incense of the Day: Apricot

Wear Something Gaudy Day

To borrow from *The Wizard of Oz*, are you a flashy witch or a somber witch in your manner of dress? No matter your personal style, today is the day to be colorful! Be it top, bottom, accessories, shoes, or jewelry (or everything!), feel free to create the most extravagant ensemble possible. It is the run-up to Halloween, and all manner of accessories are available. The purple top with the orange belt? The pumpkin socks with red shoes? The falling-leaves scarf, cauldron pin, and wand earrings? Perhaps this is the day to test-run your Halloween costume. Go crazy, have fun, and be sure to get a picture of yourself. For those who typically prefer less loud clothing, perhaps you will find it comfortable to be on the wild side for a change. For those who are usually flashy, this is the chance to really strut your stuff. Chant:

Iris, goddess of the rainbow, inspire me in my clothing choices today.

I honor you with bright colors and shiny baubles.

Emyme

 ## October 18
Friday

3rd ♊

☽ v/c 10:14 pm

Color of the Day: Coral
Incense of the Day: Cypress

Balance Bringer

The energies in the air today will likely make you reconsider how you spend your life force and where you invest your energy. Feelings and issues related to balance and your ability to maintain balance in the long term become of concern, even though this is the perfect time for you to perform magic to stabilize the balance in your life.

Spend time meditating today and truly thinking about the areas in your life where you feel balance is lacking. Ask yourself what causes this imbalance and what you can do to improve the situation. Face the north, light a blue candle, and say:

Spirits and allies, come to my side, toward balance I need a guide.

Project an image into the candle of what it would be like if balance were present in the matter. Then allow the candle to burn down completely and safely.

Devin Hunter

October 19
Saturday

3rd ♊

☽ → ♋ 6:43 am

Color of the Day: Blue
Incense of the Day: Ivy

Stop the Gossip Spell

This spell will help put a stop to gossip and slander. First, you'll need a square piece of black fabric. It's even better if the edges are frayed. You'll also need a few crumbled dry leaves, some dust, a dash of clove, a nail, and the remnants of a spider web.

Toss all the spell ingredients into the center of the fabric, and tie up the corners to form a bundle. Grasp the bundle tightly and say this charm:

Leaves, dust, clove, nail,
and spider web,

Catch and hold the lies
that are being said.

Trap the gossip in this bundle
and remove its breath.

Spirits of justice, let the
gossip die a quiet death.

Hide or hang the bundle in a secret place. The gossip will fade. When the gossip stops, bury the bundle or throw it away.

James Kambos

 October 20
Sunday

3rd ♋

Color of the Day: Orange
Incense of the Day: Hyacinth

Sukkot ends

Magickal Rapping Rhyme Writing

Today is rapper Snoop Dogg's birthday. Snoop Dogg is well known for his rhyming artistry, so much so that many other musical artists of different genres have him as a guest artist on their songs. I myself like to employ rhyming when creating simple spells and magickal workings. It adds some pizazz and is an easy way to generate magickal focus.

Today, in honor of Snoop's rhyming skills, try your hand at creating a magickal rhyme of your own! This exercise really is two bits of magick rolled into one. The first is the magickal act of creating the rhyme, and the second is its use in your spell! When you get your rhyme to where you are happy with it, be sure to record it in your magickal journal or book of shadows. Perhaps after this exercise you'll feel inspired to fill successive blank pages with magickal rhymes and poetry!

Blake Octavian Blair

October 21
Monday

3rd ♋

☽ v/c 8:39 am

4th Quarter 8:39 am

☽ → ♌ 12:29 pm

Color of the Day: White
Incense of the Day: Lily

Lavender-Mint Sereni-tea

This is a simple witches' brew to bring peace and happiness as well as prosperity and protection. Give some to everyone in your home to help promote a happy home environment.

For this tea you will need:

¼ cup lavender flowers

1 cup mint leaves

4 cups water

Add the herbs to a pot and cover with water. Stirring clockwise with a wooden spoon, enchant the brew with the following incantation:

Lavender to calm and soothe,

Leaves of mint to clear the mind,

Prosperity with both combined,

Bring happiness into my home.

Bring to a boil. Reduce the heat and simmer for about 15–20 minutes. Strain. Serve hot, or cool completely and then serve over ice. Add honey to sweeten, if desired.

Storm Faerywolf

 October 22
Tuesday

4th ♌

Color of the Day: Scarlet
Incense of the Day: Bayberry

Coconut Oil Cleanser

Coconut oil has recently experienced an upsurge in popularity, especially in skin care. When applied to the face, it has antimicrobial properties and is said to cleanse the pores. Magically, coconut is associated with purification and protection, which makes it perfect for use as a practical beauty product and a magical ointment all in one.

Place some coconut oil in a special jar, along with a piece of quartz crystal. Quartz crystal is both purifying and empowering. On the outside of the jar, paint a symbol for spiritual purification, such as an outline of a drop of water. If possible, leave your tightly lidded jar outside during a rain shower to empower it with purification energy. If this isn't possible, hold the jar under running tap water to imbue it with water's ability to vanquish negativity. Every evening before bed, wash your face by applying a small amount of the coconut oil to your skin and then rinsing it off gently. As the coconut oil removes all the dirt, grime, and makeup from the day, it also cleanses away any negative energy that has clung to you.

Kate Freuler

October 23
Wednesday

4th ♌

☽ v/c 5:14 am
☉ → ♏ 1:20 pm
☽ → ♍ 3:29 pm

Color of the Day: Brown
Incense of the Day: Honeysuckle

Send a Message

There's probably somebody you want or need to talk to. Wednesday (*mercredi* in French) is Mercury's day, so ask the fleet-footed god of communication for help.

First, determine what you want or need to tell the person with whom you need to communicate. Write it down, "speaking" clearly and courteously. Set up your altar with a blue (the color of the throat chakra = communication) candle and a clean sheet of paper.

Using this paper, fold a paper airplane. Write your name, the name Mercury, and the name of the person you want to communicate with on one side of the paper airplane. Draw arrows from your name to Mercury to the person's name. On the other side of the paper airplane, write what you want to say. Launch the paper airplane into the air. Visualize the person receiving your message and nodding. Visualize your conversation. When you finish, burn the airplane (safely) and bury the ashes outside.

Barbara Ardinger

October 24
Thursday

4th ♍

Color of the Day: Purple
Incense of the Day: Mulberry

Valuing Diversity Spell

On October 24, 1945, the United Nations ratified the UN Charter of Human Rights, which "reaffirmed faith in fundamental human rights, and dignity and worth of the human person." The Universal Declaration of Human Rights was later adopted by the UN General Assembly in Paris on December 10, 1948.

Gather a nickel, dime, quarter, and dollar coin. Canadians add a toonie, Americans a half-dollar. Whatever you buy, let these coins remind you of our diversity as a human race. Every coin is different, and each has value. Be mindful. From now on, with each purchase and every coin you receive, make your pledge to value diversity:

I am my own member state of the United Nations. I abide by the UN Charter and promote "universal respect for, and observance of, human rights and fundamental freedoms for all without distinction as to race, sex, language, or religion." So be it.

Read the charter at www.un.org/en /universal-declaration-human-rights.

Dallas Jennifer Cobb

October 25
Friday

4th ♏

☽ v/c 9:00 am

☽ → ♎ 4:20 pm

Color of the Day: Rose
Incense of the Day: Orchid

Tree Spell for Stability

People often use trees as symbols of grounding—being rooted in one place as a metaphor for stability or connecting with the earth. In addition, there's something comforting about the strength and endurance of trees, qualities people strive to cultivate. Use this spell to embody the stability of trees. They, too, can break under pressure—anything can—but they represent the ability to reach great heights while remaining connected to the earth. You can achieve what you reach for, but it's important to stay grounded.

Sit near your favorite tree (or trees) and chant:

A sigh of leaves in rush of wind,
they're stable yet they sway and bend.

Roots go deep and branches high,
growing, reaching earth and sky,
teaching us with every breeze
to learn the wisdom of the trees.

Ember Grant

 October 26
Saturday

4th ♎

Color of the Day: Indigo
Incense of the Day: Pine

Practical Tips for Every Day

The season of transition is a great time to commit to new healthful habits. SAD, or seasonal affective disorder, is a seasonal circadian condition that causes irregular moods, depression, and unpredictable sleep patterns in those who are photosensitive to the decreasing amounts of daytime light.

If the darker months of our orbit really get you down, why not start soaking up the light today? Acquire a solar therapy lamp and begin meditating for five to ten minutes a day. Use the following Latin mantra to create a continuum of light within and all around you: *Lux ad infinitum* ("Light to infinity").

This phrase's deeper meaning is that light is eternal and continually present, even if invisible.

If you can commit yourself to worshiping light throughout the season of darkness by choosing self-care and personal wellbeing, then the darkness of the season can be overcome simply by following healthy daily habits.

Estha McNevin

October 27
Sunday

4th ♎

☽ v/c 4:22 am

☽ → ♏ 4:29 pm

New Moon 11:39 pm

Color of the Day: Amber
Incense of the Day: Frankincense

Put It in a Bucket

Being witchy means being crafty, but what does one do with magickal leftovers from dolls, spells, and petition papers? How about storing them in a magickal bucket?

Many craft stores sell plastic buckets, which come in all sizes and shapes. Pick one that suits you. Have fun decorating it with witchy signs and symbols. When you have remnants from your workings, such as herbs, candle wax, papers, or hair, drop them in your magickal bucket.

Once your bucket is full, dig a hole on a dark witchy night and empty your bucket into the soil, preferably behind your home. Placing your remnants behind your home keeps your magick with you, protecting you. Cover the remnants with soil and say:

On this night and every night,
the earth keeps these things, to
her delight. She guards them
well, for no one tells, what lies
beneath the soil is hidden well!

Najah Lightfoot

 October 28
Monday

1st ♏

Color of the Day: Lavender
Incense of the Day: Clary sage

The Silver-Tongued Devil Spell

This spell takes an everyday mundane activity and transforms it into a spell for blessing our words and speech. The devil referenced here is the "man in black" or priest of the Horned God, who represents the divine and primal presence within all witches.

For this spell you will need your toothbrush and some toothpaste and some essential oil(s) of your choosing (tea tree, peppermint, and/or cinnamon are all good choices).

Ground and center. Apply toothpaste to your toothbrush and add a few drops of the oil(s) on top.

As you brush your teeth, mentally repeat the following, imagining the brush "activating" your mouth with divine presence as a bold, silver light:

Devil with the silver tongue,

I call on you to charge my words

With truth and purpose,
strength and might,

Blessed with kindness and delight.

"See" your mouth shining with divine light. Remember this as you go about your day.

Storm Faerywolf

October 29
Tuesday

1st ♏

☽ v/c 1:34 pm

☽ → ♐ 5:58 pm

Color of the Day: Red
Incense of the Day: Cedar

Ancestor Altars

At Samhain, the veil between the worlds grows thin and communication becomes easier with those who have gone beyond. That makes this the perfect time to create an ancestor altar. You can make this altar specific to one person, or it can be a general altar for all your beloved dead. They don't have to be actual ancestors, although some people do that too. Pets are fine to include as well. You can use pictures of the dead or items that symbolize them, black candles, or anything that speaks to you. You may want to put out offerings of incense, food and drink, or flowers, or anything else your dead might appreciate. In the nights leading up to Samhain, spend a few minutes at your altar communing with and sending love out to those you have lost.

Deborah Blake

October 30
Wednesday

1st ♐

Color of the Day: White
Incense of the Day: Marjoram

Invocation to Carpo

The ancient Greeks divided the seasons into spring, summer, and autumn. The three Horae (goddesses) watched over them in turn. Thallo brought the flowers of spring. Auxo increased the plant growth in summer. Carpo ripened the harvest in autumn, and then returned the land to rest until spring should come again. Here is an invocation for Carpo, suitable for a variety of autumn rituals:

Blessed be, bringer of food,

Cloud-keeper of autumn's mood.

All ripens and withers now:

Garden, orchard, field, and cow.

Hera's handmaid, full of grace,

Carpo, come and show your face.

After the ritual concludes, you may use this devocation, customarily delivered by the same person who invoked Carpo:

We give thanks for autumn's food

And the clouds of Carpo's mood.

Rite is done and over now,
Fallow field and sleeping cow.
Carpo, take our thanks with grace.
Now depart and veil your face.

                    Elizabeth Barrette

October 31
Thursday

1st ♐

☽ v/c 10:30 am
☽ → ♑ 10:38 pm

Color of the Day: Crimson
Incense of the Day: Myrrh

Samhain – halloween

halloween

Mercury in retrograde motion brings the chance for poor communication. What if this year you choose to bring your practice inward? Interact with no one, no front porch lights, no treats for the neighborhood children. Plan a Halloween movie retreat in your own home. A few musts: candles or incense, cleansing of body and viewing space, and comfortable seating. Enjoy your favorite seasonal celebration foods and beverages, healthy or not. Dress up or down. How about mulled wine, finger foods, and a pumpkin dessert? Then dive into one or more of the non-horror films of the season. A few examples: *Hocus Pocus* or *Bedknobs and Broomsticks* or maybe even *It's the Great Pumpkin, Charlie Brown* or *Practical Magic*. Hollywood provides numerous choices. *Bell Book and Candle*, anyone? Settle in for a film fest and scoff at the inconsistencies.

                    Emyme

November

The sounds of nature begin to quiet down in November, but this month is far from silent. Yes, the cheery morning birdsong of spring is gone, and crickets are no longer fiddling on warm summer afternoons, but November has its own "voices." On a frosty November morning, you'll hear a faint, faraway gabble. Raise your eyes toward the sky, and coming over the horizon, in a V formation heading south, is a flock of wild geese. The sound makes you pause and wonder: how do they know it's time to migrate? As you rake leaves, the late autumn breeze stirs them, and they softly rustle as they click and swirl up the street. Few sounds say November like the wind. It may be as gentle as a baby's breath or it may roar, carrying the weight of the coming winter as it howls in the night. During the night you can also hear November's most haunting voice: the lone hooting of an owl. Yes, this month has many voices, but every evening I hear the most comforting voice of all. That voice belongs to the crackling of burning logs as my hearth fire wards off the chill of a dark November night.

During this mysterious month, let the voices of November speak to you, igniting your imagination and your magic.

James Kambos

November 1
Friday

1st ♑

Color of the Day: White
Incense of the Day: Yarrow

All Saints' Day

Who Are Our Modern Saints?

Halfway through the first Christian millennium, there were already too many saints to have their own days. This led to the creation of All Saints' Day, which honors all saints known and unknown. (Read more online in the Catholic Encyclopedia at www.newadvent.org/cathen/01315a.htm.) We know that some saints, like Saint Brigit, are pagan goddesses or gods with new names and invented histories.

We Pagans can name our own modern saints. These are people, religious or not, who work for the rights of all people and to protect our Mother Earth and all her children. My nominations are Eleanor Roosevelt, Pete Seeger, and Nelson Mandela. Whom do you nominate?

Gather your coven, name your modern saints, and cast a circle with a purple candle for each person named. Lay photos or other symbols of these people on the altar. Honor them by singing your favorite chants. Invoke their help to inspire you to carry on their good works.

Barbara Ardinger

November 2
Saturday

1st ♑

Color of the Day: Brown
Incense of the Day: Sage

Celebration Altar

Consider creating this altar as a way to honor your ancestors and other departed souls who are dear to you. You might place photos of the deceased on your altar, but most of the space should be occupied by things that these precious souls enjoyed during life. You can include their favorite foods, favorite flowers, favorite candies, favorite colors, statues of favorite animals, or anything else you feel the departed spirit might enjoy. Take some time to enjoy each of these items as you think about the positive aspects of the person's life and its impact. Express your thanks and share your joy with the spirits who have gathered at your altar.

Melanie Marquis

November 3
Sunday

1st ⛢

☽ v/c 1:46 am

☽ → ≈ 6:19 am

Color of the Day: Yellow
Incense of the Day: Heliotrope

Daylight Saving Time
ends at 2:00 a.m.

Ending Daylight Saving Time Meditation

Last spring we pushed the clocks forward an hour. Over the summer months this gave us more time for our crops and magickal work in the sunlight. This period ends today, as we prepare to fall back—by turning the clocks back an hour.

Go outside or near a window (depending on the weather) to reflect. Sit in a comfortable position on the ground or floor, preferably. Breathe slowly and evenly. Focus your eyes softly inward, to the center of your forehead. Visualize the warmth of the sunlight collecting in this spiritual energy center. Soak in light with every breath. Breathe in and feel sunlight permeate your being. Breathe out and come to appreciate and understand the power of darkness. Feel warm, comforted, and ready to go forward, lit by the fire within.

Stephanie Rose Bird

November 4
Monday

1st ≈

2nd Quarter 5:23 am

Color of the Day: Gray
Incense of the Day: Hyssop

To Prepare the home for Spirits

Today Mercury is resting well in the sign of Scorpio, adding increased awareness of the spirit world and opening the lines of communication between our realm and those of our allies. Since the sun is also currently transiting the same sign, you are likely to find spirits in your home at this time, especially spirits of the dead.

Prepare for them by cleaning your home like you do when company is coming. Then set out a bowl of milk, a glass of wine or juice, a cup of coffee, and a few snacks. Light a white candle, and as you do so, set the space by saying:

From under and over,
From within and without,
From behind and before,
I open the door.

Spirits join me,
If you are of good will.
I've set this space
For you to fill!

Allow the candle to safely burn for several hours before extinguishing it.

Devin hunter

November 5
Tuesday

2nd ≈

☽ v/c 9:37 am

☽ → ♓ 6:08 pm

Color of the Day: Maroon
Incense of the Day: Cinnamon

Election Day (general)

The Path to Success

Today is Election Day in the United States, this time with a general election. It's a good opportunity to think about your decisions and how they lead to positive or negative outcomes.

To cast a spell for success, you need a candle (gold, silver, or purple), a small square of cloth (same colors), a stone (alexandrite, sunstone, or lodestone), and an herb (lemon, cinnamon, or clover). Consider your options and choose the ones that best resonate with your goal. Lay them all out on your altar. Light the candle and speak about your objective, what you need to succeed. Lay the stone on the cloth and cover it with the herb. Visualize the candlelight infusing them with energy. Tie the corners of the cloth together. Let the candle burn out.

Carry the charm with you. Touch it when you need to choose the path to success.

Elizabeth Barrette

November 6
Wednesday

2nd ♓

Color of the Day: Topaz
Incense of the Day: Lavender

Wish Upon a Star

The Taurid meteor shower is happening in both the Northern and Southern Hemispheres at this time. Sightings with the naked eye require patience—and comfort. Where I live, we bundle up and recline in the back yard, where there is less ambient light. Caution: if it's warm enough, you may doze off and miss it. Sometimes the weather is too cold or cloudy. Sometimes a sighting happens by accident. The best sighting I ever experienced was when I was driving very early in the morning, waiting for a green light, and several meteors crossed my field of vision. Spectacular!

Plan a family viewing or be an audience of one. Wear appropriate clothing and provide soft items on which to recline, plus maybe binoculars and a telescope. Prepare your "shooting star" wishes. Settle in for one of the most amazing sights ever. Chant:

Streaks across the sky, hear my plea:

(Insert wish here.)

Delight and awe accompany thee!

Emyme

November 7
Thursday

2nd ♓

☽ v/c 8:13 pm

Color of the Day: Turquoise
Incense of the Day: Balsam

Water Magic

Depending on where you live, the water element might be manifesting itself as rain, snow, or fog at this time of year. Or you might live someplace where water is scarce. But no matter where you are, you can do this simple water magic. If it is precipitating outside in any form, set out a bowl to catch it. Otherwise, just use tap water, which came from the sky and the ground somewhere. Sit in a quiet room and scoop up a little water on your fingertips. Anoint first the top of your head, then your forehead, then your chest, then your abdomen. As you do so, say:

Bless my spirit with this water.

Bless my mind and my heart.

Bless the core of my body,

Made too of water, that is the source of all life.

Thank you, water, for all that you do.

Deborah Blake

 ## November 8
Friday

2nd ♓

☽ → ♈ 6:49 am

Color of the Day: Coral
Incense of the Day: Vanilla

Your Own Love Song

On this day in 1947, American singer-songwriter Minnie Riperton was born. She is most famous for her hit single "Lovin' You." Later in life, she continued to tour and record despite being diagnosed with aggressive breast cancer and given just months to live. Let's let such talent, strength, and tenacity be an inspiration to us.

Today, try your hand at writing a song, chant, or poem about something you love, in honor of her hit song's title "Lovin' You." Love is about more than romance, so really think about something you have a deep passion for. Get a pen and some paper. Set a piece of rose quartz near you and light a pink candle for a loving inspiration boost. After your writing session, safely snuff out the candle. When you're finished with your own piece of musical love magic, find a friend you're willing to share it with, and do so. You too can inspire others with your passions!

Blake Octavian Blair

November 9
Saturday

2nd ♈

Color of the Day: Blue
Incense of the Day: Sandalwood

Take a Break

Halloween is over, Samhain has passed, and the Day of the Dead is gone. After all the revelry, we may be a bit worn out.

Today, take a break. Although we are gearing down, the rest of the world is just getting started for the upcoming holidays. Say no to the world, just for today.

Give yourself permission not to answer your phone, check email, or log into social media accounts. If someone comes to your door, pretend you're not home!

Stay in your pajamas. Go out without combing your hair. If that bothers you, put on a hat. Watch favorite movies or read a book. Be kind to yourself, because before you know it, the wheel will turn and you'll be back, running here and there, to and fro, again!

Najah Lightfoot

November 10
Sunday

2nd ♈

☽ v/c 9:00 am

☽ → ♉ 6:18 pm

Color of the Day: Gold
Incense of the Day: Eucalyptus

Mercury Retrograde Communication Spell

This spell aims to remove blocks that would prevent us from effectively communicating our desires during Mercury retrograde. Here we will express ourselves on paper and use that as a means to distill our intentions and convey them magically to the intended recipient.

You will need:

• A pen and paper

• Dried lavender flowers

• Dried mint

• A blue candle

• A cauldron or fire-safe ash pot

Ground and center. Focus on the person (or persons) for whom this communication is necessary. Call out their name three times. Now write down whatever it is that you wish to convey to them. Express your absolute needs and boundaries, whatever it is that you need them to understand. Sprinkle the paper with the dried herbs and fold it in half, three times. Carefully burn the paper in the flame of the candle and then put it in the cauldron or pot. Scatter the ashes to the wind.

Now, when communicating further on this issue, remember the clarity with which you wrote, and draw from that experience to better elucidate your thoughts.

Storm Faerywolf

NOTES:

November 11
Monday

2nd ♉

Color of the Day: White
Incense of the Day: Neroli

Veterans Day –
Remembrance Day (Canada)

Winter Travel Advisory Withstanding

Here in Montana, we're used to driving in some pretty unforgiving weather conditions. Early and often we learn the wisdom of on-rig support, from glow sticks to rough-and-ready food packs; indeed it is wise to travel with a kind of preparedness in all seasons when venturing out into the wild lands. Amongst our chains and Army-Navy survival food packs, you'll also find an emergency spell kit with the following items:

- Candle
- Matches/lighter
- Compass
- Mirror
- Small boline blade
- Copy of the book *Be Here Now* by Ram Dass

If you encounter accident, injury, or misdirection, have a contingency travel plan in case emergency services need to search your vehicle for clues of your identity or whereabouts. Use the compass to get your bearings; pray to the direction you find yourself in. Envision your topical knowledge of where you are, and stay put for as long as you can. Use the boline to gather kindling and small shrub wood. Use the candle and matches to light a fire. If you are distressed, evoke the elements and observe a solution, or combat stress by reading from the monumental and visionary work of Baba Ram Dass.

Estha McNevin

November 12
Tuesday

2nd ♉

🌕 Full Moon 8:34 am

☽ v/c 10:48 am

Color of the Day: Scarlet

Incense of the Day: Ginger

A Full Moon Spell to Increase Psychic Powers

The November full moon, also known as the Frost Moon, is a potent time to perform spells to increase psychic abilities. For this spell you'll need a small glass or crystal sphere. Hold the sphere up so the moon is visible through it. If it's a cloudy night, face toward the direction of the moon. Hold the image of the moon with your eye and say:

> Frost Moon, guardian of the Mysteries,
>
> Bestow upon me the gift of prophecy.
>
> Frost Moon, crown jewel of the November night,
>
> Bless me with the gift of second sight.

Thus, you've charged your sphere with the psychic energy of the November full moon. This is now a sacred magical tool. Keep it wrapped in fine black fabric, such as silk or velvet. Let no one else touch it. Place it on your altar when you work with any divining tool.

James Kambos

November 13
Wednesday

3rd ♉

☽ → ♊ 3:46 am

Color of the Day: Yellow

Incense of the Day: Bay laurel

Onion Spell to Reveal the Truth

This spell is to be performed when you know someone is being dishonest about something important but their manipulation is keeping you and others from the truth. This spell takes several days to complete and should be begun today, during the waning moon.

Cut the top off an onion. Insert a pin or sewing needle directly into the center core and push it all the way down. This pin represents the truth. Peel the first layer off the outside of the onion. Visualize a barrier being broken in your situation; see yourself getting closer to finding out what you need to know. Each night at the same time, peel another layer off the onion. By the time you get to the pin at the center, the truth will be revealed. Be warned: it may not be what you expected!

Kate Freuler

November 14
Thursday

3rd ♊

Color of the Day: Green
Incense of the Day: Mulberry

Cheer Up!

Starting about mid-November, gloomy weather and the prospect of family holidays can make us depressed. All those old family arguments around the dinner table… or maybe we're not even invited. Which is worse? Our minds fill up with resentments and—whoa! Stop that. It's not healthy.

What to do? Occupy your mind with cheerier, more useful thoughts:

1. Recite a mantra like *Om Tare Tuttare Ture Soha*, or maybe turn it into a song. Recite or sing it while you're driving.

2. Read Dion Fortune's *The Mystical Qabalah* and learn the names and meanings of the ten sephiroth: Kether, Chokmah, Binah, Chesed, Geburah, Tiphareth, Netzach, Hod, Yesod, and Malkuth. Learn to recite them up and down the Tree of Life.

3. Sing Deena Metzger's goddess chant: *Isis, Astarte, Diana, Hecate, Demeter, Kali, Inanna.*

If you're working on remembering which sephira goes where or which goddess comes next, you won't have time to be depressed. Cheer up!

Barbara Ardinger

November 15
Friday

3rd ♊

☽ v/c 6:40 am
☽ → ♋ 11:15 am

Color of the Day: Pink
Incense of the Day: Mint

Affirmation to Banish Negative Emotions

We all have those days when we feel down, overly critical of ourselves, or unappreciated. Don't let those negative emotions deceive you. Use this spell to banish them and restore your confidence. All you need for this spell is a blanket.

Find a comfortable place to sit and wrap yourself in the blanket. Make yourself as cozy as possible. Visualize the blanket as a reassuring hug or a pat on the back.

Chant:

Dismiss all the worry,
don't let it hold sway.

Start over tomorrow,
another new day.

Can't beat myself up,
just release the care.

With these gentle words
I no longer despair.

Follow up by doing something you enjoy or pampering yourself. You deserve it.

Ember Grant

November 16
Saturday

3rd ♋

Color of the Day: Black
Incense of the Day: Patchouli

Restoring the Calm Spell

Use this spell to restore calm and balance when you find yourself in circumstances of chaos and annoyance. Fill a wide-mouthed glass with water. Sprinkle on a large quantity of black pepper as you think about all the things in your life that are currently causing you irritation. Now take a deep breath, exhaling across the top of the glass as you squeeze a single drop of dishwashing liquid into the water. As the pepper quickly flees from the soap due to changes in surface tension, envision your irritations being driven away just as swiftly from your own sphere of influence.

Melanie Marquis

November 17
Sunday

3rd ♋

☽ v/c 3:14 pm
☽ → ♌ 4:57 pm

Color of the Day: Orange
Incense of the Day: Juniper

Make a Wish

Tonight and tomorrow are peak nights for the annual Leonid meteor shower, occurring from November 5 to 30 in 2019. Up to fifteen meteors per hour will be visible to the naked eye. Go outdoors, in the dark, after midnight. Find the constellation of Leo, where the meteors radiate from. A meteor is matter broken off an asteroid or comet that burns up upon entering the earth's atmosphere. The "shooting stars" effect lasts for a few seconds or up to a minute.

Like a kid, invoke the magic of the stars. When you see a meteor trail, repeat the age-old rhyme with a minor change:

Star light, star bright,
this meteor I see tonight,

I wish I may, I wish I might,
have this wish I wish tonight.

Make a wish. Or stay out for an hour and make up to fifteen wishes on the bright meteor trails streaking across the sky.

Dallas Jennifer Cobb

November 18
Monday

3rd ♌

Color of the Day: Ivory
Incense of the Day: Narcissus

Apple Cider for Friendship

Today is National Apple Cider Day in the United States. Apples have a long-standing association with love and healing. I'm also a big proponent of the importance of acknowledging that there are many types of love aside from the romantic kind. We need loving familial relationships and friendships as well.

Today, prepare or procure a couple cups of hot apple cider. Have a sitdown with a beloved friend or family member and nurture your relationship over this magickal drink. A cuppa with a loved one is bonding time, especially over this drink made from the magickal apple! If your friend is of the magickal persuasion as well, try out this blessing over your ciders:

Magickal apple! Powerful brew!

Mulled and steeped with care

As good friendships do!

Warm and healing,

As both a friend and a
cuppa should be.

Friends and cider together, blessed be!
Blake Octavian Blair

 November 19
Tuesday

3rd ♌

☽ v/c 4:11 pm

4th Quarter 4:11 pm

☽ → ♍ 8:54 pm

Color of the Day: Red
Incense of the Day: Basil

Gratitude Spell

Those of us who live in the United States celebrate Thanksgiving later this month, but the truth is, the "giving thanks" part of the holiday often gets lost in the commotion of the day. So why not take a minute today to do this simple spell for gratitude, no matter where you live? No matter how difficult life might be, no matter what struggles you face, there are always things to be grateful for. Light a candle and sit quietly for a moment, thinking about all the parts of your life that are worthy of appreciation. Then say this spell:

God and Goddess, I thank you

For the good things, which lift me up,

And the bad, which teach
me and make me strong.

Thank you for [list the things
you are grateful for]

And for all the gifts that you give me.

I am grateful.
Deborah Blake

November 20
Wednesday

4th ♏

Color of the Day: Brown
Incense of the Day: Honeysuckle

Intolerance and Ignorance of the Craft

It is a constant source of wonder and amusement to see and hear what non-Wiccan folk (Muggles?) think they know about the old ways. Education and "approval" have grown, but we still have a ways to go. The ignorance and intolerance and derision and exclusion only serve to showcase/highlight the inclusion and welcoming ways of all earth-based paths in our community. Just look at some of the factions: kitchen, hedge, fey, solitary, coven, eclectic. Unless there is bodily harm involved, all negative words, thoughts, and actions must be allowed to flow over and pass by us. Greet the negative with a smile and kind words and keep to the creed:

My beliefs serve me well in this world.

I choose my path.

An it harm none, do what you will.

Emyme

 ## November 21
Thursday

4th ♏

☽ v/c 10:31 pm

☽ → ♎ 11:20 pm

Color of the Day: Purple
Incense of the Day: Jasmine

Cry in a Graveyard

Did you know there are graveyards and cemeteries that were intentionally created as parks so visitors would feel comfortable sitting there for a while? Not all graveyards and cemeteries are creepy, scary places. Some are actually quite soothing and beautiful.

If you're feeling blue today, try spending some time in your favorite graveyard. Graveyards and cemeteries are some of the few places where you can cry to your heart's content, uninterrupted. No one will give you strange looks for weeping in a graveyard.

When you enter the graveyard, be sure to throw some coins to the spiritual gatekeeper who watches over the gates. When you leave, say thank you to the graveyard for taking your tears and soothing your heart. Take a different route back when you leave the graveyard so your sorrows won't follow you home.

Najah Lightfoot

November 22

Friday

4th ♎

☉ → ♐ 9:59 am

Color of the Day: Rose
Incense of the Day: Alder

The Jar of Bitter-Sweet

Here is a spell for sweetening up a stressful or bitter situation. You will need:

- A small lemon
- A permanent marker
- A small to medium-sized jar with a metal lid
- Honey
- Some dried or fresh lavender
- A white candle in a holder

Empower the lemon to be a connection to what is causing you stress by creating a sigil and drawing this with permanent marker on the peel. Allow to dry. Fill the jar halfway with honey, then add some lavender. Insert the lemon, then cover with honey to fill the jar completely. Scoop up some honey on your finger and put in your mouth so you can taste it. Say:

Honey, sweet upon my tongue,

Sweeten now the bitter one.

Into darkness shine your light,

Bring me peace, make all things bright.

Close the lid tightly and burn the candle on top of it safely. Burn a new candle on top of it each week and speak the charm aloud.

Storm Faerywolf

November 23
Saturday

4th ♎

☽ v/c 9:49 pm

Color of the Day: Indigo
Incense of the Day: Magnolia

Lonely Is the Night

November nights can be long and lonely if you haven't found that special someone. To begin this spell to find love, rub two red taper candles with almond oil. Put them in holders and light them. Slowly pull the candles toward you. As you do this, begin speaking these words:

Candles, burn away my
loneliness in the night.

Candles, bring love to
me with your light.

With this spell, I ask that
love comes into sight.

Candles, burn away my
loneliness in the night.

Let the candles burn out safely. Remove them from their holders and keep them in an attractive box. Be open to any sign that romance is coming your way.

James Kambos

November 24
Sunday

4th ♎

☽ → ♏ 12:58 am

Color of the Day: Yellow
Incense of the Day: Almond

Reed Month Vision Quest

In the Celtic ogham, trees are celebrated and revered. This is the end of Reed Month on the Celtic tree calendar. Reed (a tree-like plant) grows in and near the water of wetlands and gracefully yields to the ebb and flow of tides and winds. It's a purifying and clarifying plant that is useful on vision quests, as it provides direction.

For this vision quest, obtain some Celtic music featuring wind instruments made from reeds, such as flutes. Play the reed music, letting its haunting beauty evoke ancient times, and your place within them.

Get in a comfortable position. Focus entirely on your breath for a few minutes. Inhale on a count of eight, then exhale slowly on an eight count. Continue for eight minutes, until you are relaxed.

Slowly come back into yourself—wiggle your toes and shake out your hands. Open your eyes gradually. How do you feel? What did you see? Take notes. Continue this journey next year during Celtic Reed Month.

Stephanie Rose Bird

November 25
Monday

4th ♏

☽ v/c 12:30 pm

Color of the Day: Silver
Incense of the Day: Rosemary

Ear Charms to Improve Listening

Earrings with bells are of ancient origin. The Kashmir Valley inhabitants of northwestern India date them back to the third-century-BCE Indus River, and they still believe that these jhumka bobbles are sacred to the goddess Parvati. Evocative of Shakti, the force of sound and creation, they symbolize the Himalayan divine creatrix of all life. Anointing and wearing these charms on days when compassion, understanding, and listening are your goals will bring you success.

Acquire a pair of jhumka bell-shaped earrings that make a soft, soothing noise when they move. Wash both of them gently in black salt. Anoint them with seven drops each of saffron oil and rose oil to aromatically inspire listening skills that open like roses in the dew. Every time the bells on your jhumkas jingle, remember to listen for Shakti. These charms are especially favored around family holidays and are a common gift between sisters and friends.

Estha McNevin

 November 26
Tuesday

4th ♏

☽ → ♐ 3:11 am

New Moon 10:06 am

Color of the Day: Black
Incense of the Day: Bayberry

Jupiter Clarity Spell

Currently the sun, the new moon, and Jupiter are all stationed in Sagittarius, making for some pretty potent energy. This is a time when your internal world is begging to be set free and allowed to manifest, but before it can do so, you must first find the words to describe what it is you are experiencing and what it is you want to manifest. Using the power of Jupiter (which rules Sagittarius), we can find those words.

Light a gold candle and place it before you. In your mind's eye, draw the sigil for Jupiter (♃) and envision it entering the candle flame. Focus on the tension you feel internally, and send it into the candle flame as well. Take a few breaths and then visualize the symbol for Jupiter leaving the flame and entering your throat chakra. Spend the next few days meditating and journaling about anything that comes up.

Devin Hunter

November 27
Wednesday

1st ♏ ♐

Color of the Day: White
Incense of the Day: Marjoram

Vacation Spell

Thinking of planning a vacation? Today is Wednesday and a brand-new waxing moon—a perfect day to cast a spell to help manifest your dream holiday.

Hermes is the Greek god of transition, travel, and crossing boundaries, and is said to be able to move freely between this world and the afterlife. A symbol of Hermes is the winged sandal: what better image to symbolize you taking flight on a holiday than that?

For this spell you will need some yellow felt and thread, a feather, and a small toy doll's shoe (plastic is fine).

Cut a small rectangle out of the felt, and sew the feather and shoe inside of it like a sachet. As you do so, see yourself enjoying your dream vacation, no matter how fanciful or far away. At dusk or dawn (times of transition and movement), tuck the charm away with your luggage or with the clothing you'd wear on your holiday to carry your intentions off to the gods of travel.

Kate Freuler

November 28
Thursday

1st ♏ ♐

☽ v/c 5:50 am
☽ → ♑ 7:33 am

Color of the Day: Crimson
Incense of the Day: Myrrh

Thanksgiving Day

Thanksgiving Gratitude Spell

This is Thanksgiving Day, a time of gratitude. In many families, people gather together for an enormous feast in thanks for what they have. You can take advantage of this energy for your own benefit while helping others at the same time.

For this spell you will need a green candle and some donations. They can be nonperishable canned goods, coats, cash—whatever your local charities say they need. Light the candle. Gather your donations together and recite over them a list of things you feel grateful for. Then say:

I bless these gifts with abundance. May everyone who receives them go on to gain whatever they need in a manner that seems good to them. All that I do returns to me times three.

Allow the candle to burn down safely.

After the holiday is over, turn in your donations.

Elizabeth Barrette

November 29
Friday

1st ♑

☽ v/c 10:57 pm

Color of the Day: Purple
Incense of the Day: Thyme

Spell for Creativity

To foster inspiration and creativity, no matter what your outlet is, try this spell. You'll need several bay leaves. Dried ones from the spice rack are fine.

Bay (*Laurus nobilis*) was revered in ancient Greece and Rome. The herb was dedicated to the god Apollo. It is also said that the oracles at Delphi chewed bay leaves to induce prophetic visions. To give your own powers a boost, first charge the bay leaves with this dedication:

*I celebrate creative art
and dedicate these leaves
to help express what's in my heart
and what I can achieve.*

*Prophecy and poetry,
music, paint, and dance,
increase the skills I cultivate,
my craft to be enhanced.*

Burn the bay leaves as incense while you work. Sleep with one under your pillow at night.

Ember Grant

November 30
Saturday

1st ♑

☽ → ♒ 3:13 pm

Color of the Day: Blue
Incense of the Day: Ivy

Small Is Better Affirmation

In the US, the Saturday after Thanksgiving is celebrated as Small Business Saturday to support and promote this vital part of the economy. Since 2010, Small Business Saturday has celebrated the sector that provides approximately 66 percent of all new jobs and 54 percent of all US sales.

Today, be a conscious consumer. Vote with your dollars. Spend in a way that expresses your deeply held belief in community. Go out of your way to shop with local, family-based entrepreneurs and small businesses. Bypass the big-box stores today and put your money into the hands of people in your community who run their own business. Know that your purchase makes a difference in the community, in your local economy, and in the sustainability of local people. Each time you hand over money, affirm:

Small is better. I vote with my money. I vote for people and small business sustainability.

Dallas Jennifer Cobb

December

December features a palette of cool colors: white snow, silver icicles, evergreen, and, of course, blue—the bright cerulean sky on a clear, cold winter's day, or the deep navy velvet of the darkening nights, culminating on the longest night of the year, the winter solstice. This hue is reflected in December's birthstones: turquoise, zircon, tanzanite, and lapis. The notion of a stone representing each month has been linked to ayurvedic beliefs that suggest correspondences between the planets and crystals. It wasn't until the eighteenth century that associating stones with a birth month became a popular practice in the Western world.

Even if you weren't born in December, you can still tap into the power of this month's special stones. Zircon increases bone stability, which is good for moving over icy terrain. Use turquoise, a rain-making stone, to summon snow. Turquoise also heals and brings peace. Engage tanzanite's powers for psychic visions for the impending new year. Lapis—the mirror of the winter night sky, and a stone that can be found in the breastplate of the high priest—brings wisdom and awareness.

Natalie Zaman

December 1
Sunday

1st ♒

Color of the Day: Amber
Incense of the Day: Marigold

Aleister Crowley's Death Day Observance

On this day in 1947, Aleister Crowley, one of the greatest occult minds of the twentieth century, died. Today we remember him by celebrating his works and contributions to the craft and by holding a small vigil in his honor. We do this by lighting a red candle in the west, which has his name inscribed into the sides. Light the candle and chant his name several times until you feel a calmness fill the space around you. Then recite this piece from his poem "In Memoriam," from his 1898 book *Songs of the Spirit*:

> *The spirit, through the vision of clouds rifted,*
>
> *Soars quick and clear.*
>
> *Even so, the mists that roll o'er earth are riven,*
>
> *The spirit flashes forth from mortal sight,*
>
> *And, flaming through the viewless space, is given*
>
> *A robe of light.*

Allow the candle to burn out completely and safely.

Devin Hunter

December 2
Monday

1st ≈

☽ v/c 7:27 am

Color of the Day: Lavender
Incense of the Day: Clary sage

Quiet Ties

During the holidays, everything cranks up to a higher intensity. For extroverts, this is a ton of fun, but for introverts, not so much. Some people with special needs also feel pressured. That can slop a lot of unpleasant energy over your personal space. Happily, you can help keep the holidays fun for your friends and family.

First, encourage people to leave their crud at the door. In mundane space, use a doormat and a "Please wipe your feet" sign; clean the mat frequently. In Pagan space, you can put a smudge stick and/or feather fan at the door.

Provide a tranquil space for people to get away from the ruckus during large rituals, parties, or other events. A spare room or out-of-the-way corner will do. Offer quiet activities such as magazines, a basket of fidgets, Tarot cards, board games, puzzles, etc.

Encourage people to relax and blow off negative vibes. It helps.

Elizabeth Barrette

December 3
Tuesday

1st ≈

☽ → ♓ 2:11 am

Color of the Day: Gray
Incense of the Day: Ginger

Abundant Food Spell

Use this spell to help ensure that your food stores never run out. Prepare several large jars or canisters full of dried beans, coffee, pastas, or grains. Place a clean, clear quartz crystal and a piece of jade in each container. Be sure the stones are natural and not lab-created, as they have more power when formed over time in nature. Inscribe the lid of each container with a plus symbol or a multiplication sign. Whenever you take something out of one of the jars, imagine that jar refilling itself. Add more to your stores frequently, as soon and as often as you are able.

Melanie Marquis

December 4
Wednesday

1st ♓

2nd Quarter 1:58 am

Color of the Day: Yellow
Incense of the Day: Lilac

Pet Blessing Spell

For those of us who share our lives and homes with animals, they are often more than merely pets. My cats are friends, family, and love personified (not to mention one familiar). Here is a blessing for your beloved furbabies:

Bast and Hecate, Horned God too,

Bless the animals of this house.

Keep them safe and healthy,

Calm and happy,

And out of trouble, please,

For they are your creatures and the treasures of my heart.

Bless these animals.

So mote it be.

Deborah Blake

December 5
Thursday

2nd ♓

☽ v/c 3:15 am ♏

☽ → ♈ 2:44 pm

Color of the Day: White
Incense of the Day: Clove

Cast Away the Darkness

At this time of year, many people don hats and coats, while others are snow-birding, heading to places where blue skies and azure oceans rule the day. Some revel in the dark days and nights of winter, while others can't wait to escape the snow and cold.

If winter brings on seasonal affective disorder, otherwise known as SAD, and your pocketbook won't support a vacation, you can easily bring the light of the sun into your life with a daylight bulb.

A daylight bulb is different from an ordinary light bulb. A daylight bulb emits a frequency of light that is close to that of natural light on a sunny day. Bring in the light of the sun with this little incantation:

The power of the sun shines strong and bright,

Its magick contained within the daylight.

This little bulb brings the light to me,

Effortlessly and continuously!

Najah Lightfoot

December 6

Friday

2nd ♈

Color of the Day: Pink
Incense of the Day: Rose

Speak Up Incantation

In 1989 in Montreal, Quebec, fourteen young women were murdered simply because they were women. The National Day of Remembrance and Action on Violence was instituted across Canada in 1991 to remember the victims and to take action against gender-based violence. Because gender-based violence is woven intrinsically into our culture, and widely represented in popular media, we often encounter it and feel silenced and slighted. Today, let's claim the right to live free of violence. Speak up.

Place your fingertips on your throat, and empower yourself:

I use my voice and speak out clearly,

I defend the rights that I hold dearly,

I speak up and take a stand,

For freedom from violence throughout the land.

I speak my truth from deep within me,

Because silence equals complicity.

Silence equals complicity.

Practice the skill of calmly speaking truth to "power." All women deserve to live safe and free.

Dallas Jennifer Cobb

December 7
Saturday

2nd ♈

☽ v/c 10:01 am

Color of the Day: Brown
Incense of the Day: Rue

Sabago Rite

Sabago is the Spanish word for Saturday, which is today. It is derived from *sabbath*, or day of rest. Generally we keep busy as Witches. Today, I invite you to experience pure, unadulterated rest for the entire day. Begin your day like this:

Clear your calendar. Reschedule appointments if you must.

Grab your favorite CD or tune in to your most peaceful playlist.

Light blue candles (for peace and relaxation) in the bathroom. Drop some pink rose petals and rose oil into the tub. Undress and relax.

Spend the rest of the day unwinding. Do not make plans and limit any conversation.

This day is for you to heal, replenish, and nurture your soul.

Stephanie Rose Bird

December 8
Sunday

2nd ♈

☽ → ♉ 2:29 am

Color of the Day: Gold
Incense of the Day: Juniper

Magic Box

Magic is the flux and flow of Paganism. It raises energy in rituals and charges spells. It's always nice to have a little extra. Today, work a spell to attract more magic into your life.

First, you need a pretty box. Wood or stone work well for natural magic, glass for technomagic, and metal for both. Avoid insulating materials, such as silk or plastic.

Next, take a square of paper and draw arrows from each corner so they meet in the center. Place this in the bottom of the box for attraction.

Now add symbols of magic. Good stones include amber, carnelian, garnet, hawk's eye, lapis, and selenite. Choose herbs such as allspice, bergamot, cardamom pods, whole cloves, dragon's blood, frangipani, lemon peel, patchouli, or star anise. Also add any images that represent magic for you.

Visualize power flowing into the box. Close it and keep it on your altar.

Elizabeth Barrette

December 9

Monday

2nd ☿

☽ v/c 8:13 pm

Color of the Day: Silver
Incense of the Day: Lily

The Lure of Lore

We are creeping toward the Christmas and New Year holidays, the Twelfth Night and Three Kings festivities—the time of year when many families hunker down around the table and tell stories. Folk tales and fairy stories have been around since language began. Worldwide, the classics enjoy alternative plots and characters. As group entertainment, might I suggest a collective story-writing experience in which no witch is evil (because we know we are not!). Provide paper and writing instruments for each family member. Choose a story, and have everyone contribute. Even the youngest can draw illustrations. Set the timer, have everyone read their ideas out loud, and then work to combine them into an interesting and personal take on a classic. Edit, polish, and print copies for everyone. Abracadabra! A wonderful holiday memory has been created, a tradition begun.

Emyme

December 10

Tuesday

2nd ☿

☽ → ♊ 11:47 am

Color of the Day: Red
Incense of the Day: Ylang-ylang

Crystal Reflections

Crystals are sacred beings. Although they are detached from their source, the Earth Mother, their connection is strong. Crystals never lose their connection to the spiritual and the divine.

Find a crystal that calls to you. Sit quietly with it. Hold it. Look at it. Stare at its facets, sides, top, and bottom. Gaze deeply into the crystal. Close your eyes and allow it to speak to you. As thoughts and images form within your mind, be one with them.

When you feel ready, open your eyes. Thank your crystal and keep it in a place where you can look at it every day. Allow yourself to build a practice of simply sitting with it. Let your crystal be a guide into peacefulness and reflection.

Najah Lightfoot

December 11
Wednesday

2nd ♊

Color of the Day: Topaz
Incense of the Day: Bay laurel

Communicating with a Gnome

This spell will assist you in contacting a gnome: an earth elemental. Typically, these beings provide strength, steadfastness, endurance, and the ability of transmutation. Invoke them when you feel weak, unruly, or in danger of being led astray.

You will need a black candle and a simple rock large enough to at least nearly fill the palm of your hand.

Face the north, or the direction your tradition associates with the earth element. Ground and center. Place the candle on your altar, with the rock in front of it so that from your vantage point the rock completely obscures the candle flame. Enter a trance and gaze at the rock so that you can see the light of the candle around it. Call to the gnomes—the conscious beings of earth—to appear before you:

Creatures of the silent earth,

Reveal here to me your form.

Look into the stone with the Witch's eye: your inner sight. Allow the gnomes to reveal themselves to you. Once they have, you may commune with them as you wish.

Storm Faerywolf

December 12
Thursday

2nd ♊

☽ v/c 12:12 am

Full Moon 12:12 am

☽ → ♋ 6:23 pm

Color of the Day: Purple
Incense of the Day: Nutmeg

Dispel Illusions

Begin by arranging white candles of any shape or size on a mirror. Just use what you have available. Leave room in the center of the mirror. In that space, place the Moon card from a Tarot deck, if you have one. If you don't have this card, simply draw a full moon on a piece of paper and use that.

The Moon card is traditionally said to represent intuition, dreams, uncertainty, and illusion. Use this spell to help refine your powers of intuition and perception. Let the power of the full moon increase your understanding that you may not always see the total picture. Let this card remind you to look closely but also to trust your intuition. We can't rely solely on our intuition or on what we see—we need a blend of both.

Light the candles and chant:

Reflect the truth, help me see
Beyond mirage and mystery.
Let illusions be dispelled,
Intuition be upheld.
Let the moonlight be my guide,
Revealing where the truth can hide.

Ember Grant

December 13

Friday

3rd ♋

Color of the Day: Coral
Incense of the Day: Cypress

Make Your home into an Altar

Technically, the space in which a saint—or a Pagan—lives is called a shrine. But that smacks of sanctimony, so let's just turn a room into an altar. The four walls become a rectangular circle decorated with symbols of the elements. Make adjustments for architecture (doors, windows) you cannot change. Here are a few decorative suggestions:

East, air: Move at least one of your bookcases to this wall. Add decorative birds (I have an origami passenger pigeon), a witch flying on her broom, a glass "full" of air, a fluffy white feather, or a beautiful Victorian fan.

South, fire: A solar wheel, a candelabra with red candles, a Brigid's cross, sunflowers, glass rocks (especially red or orange)

West, water: Mermaids, an aquarium, shells and beach glass, a plant growing in water

North, earth: Houseplants, geodes, other largish rocks

Now stand in the center and cast your circle. You are the living altar.

Barbara Ardinger

December 14
Saturday

3rd ♋

☽ v/c 10:57 am

☽ → ♌ 10:56 pm

Color of the Day: Blue
Incense of the Day: Magnolia

A Key to Protection

Saturdays are under Hecate's care. Today, let's work with her to create a protection talisman using a key, an item commonly associated with her. Use this talisman when the stray energies flying around you are getting to be a bit much to tolerate. Find yourself a key and a length of cord. It needs to be a key you will not use for any other function or purpose. A modern or antique key will work equally well. Light a candle to Hecate, attach the cord to the key so that it may be worn as a necklace, and place the key next to the candle. Recite:

Goddess Hecate, guardian of witches,

Your dark cloak of protection

I do invoke!

A key to unlock these mysteries,

Enchant and instill.

I'll wear it around my neck

So that with your protection I shall fill!

So mote it be!

Allow the candle to safely burn down and then wear your talisman as needed.

Blake Octavian Blair

December 15
Sunday

3rd ♌

Color of the Day: Yellow
Incense of the Day: Hyacinth

Sugarplum Dreamtime Elixir Tea

For a fun family-friendly faery spell, make your own sugarplum dreamtime tea with the ones you love most. This brew takes our dreams to that land of fantasy and wonder, making bedtime a faery ritual to share stories honoring the light and warmth we create just by being together.

In an airtight glass container, mix together ⅓ cup each of dried chamomile, diced prunes, and local honey. Add 7 drops of rose oil to appease Titania, the queen of the fae, the mother to all sprites and wee little ones. Brew by combining 2 teaspoons of this elixir to 1 cup of boiled milk. To be assured of adventure and joy as you dream, sip this healthful warm tea just before bedtime and delightfully share a wee cup or two with your house faeries.

May you be blessed with glowing dreams of the springtime fae to warm your long winter nights.

Estha McNevin

 December 16
Monday

3rd ♌

☽ v/c 5:10 pm

Color of the Day: White
Incense of the Day: Rosemary

Freezing Spell to Stop Gossip

Write down a rumor you want to put a stop to on a small slip of paper. Roll it up as small as possible. Put it in a plastic cup or bottle and cover it with water completely.

Hold the cup or bottle in your hand and say:

Frozen solid, icy cold,

Stop this story from being told.

Place the cup or bottle in the freezer overnight and let it freeze solid. Leave it there until the gossip dies down or the situation passes, then dump it out and recycle the materials.

If you live in a cold part of the world, you can freeze the bottle outside instead of in the freezer.

Kate Freuler

December 17
Tuesday

3rd ♌

☽ → ♍ 2:16 am

Color of the Day: Scarlet
Incense of the Day: Cedar

Wishes Granted Divination

Use this divination to see which of your wishes is most likely to be granted the soonest. Write each of your wishes on a small slip of paper, and put these in the bottom of a large mixing bowl. Place them face down and mix them up so that you won't know which wish is which. Fill a pitcher with warm water, and slowly pour the water into the bowl. Watch carefully and note which paper is the first to rise to the top of the bowl. If more than one paper floats up to the surface simultaneously, choose the one that is nearest you. The first wish to rise to the top will be the first wish to come to fruition.

Melanie Marquis

December 18
Wednesday

3rd ♍

4th Quarter 11:57 pm

Color of the Day: Brown
Incense of the Day: Honeysuckle

Home Protection Spell

As we settle into winter, this is a good time to do a spell for protection on your home or apartment. It is natural, no matter what the climate, to retreat inward during the shorter, darker days, so it is good to make sure your "cave" is safe and secure. Light a black or white candle, and place a ribbon or piece of yarn around it in a circle to symbolize the circle of protection covering your home. If you want, burn some sage or some rosemary incense. Say this spell:

*Protect this home and
those who dwell in it.*

Keep it safe from harm or mishap,

Bad weather or ill intent.

Protect this space and make it a refuge

Full of good energy,

Secure and blessed.

So mote it be.

Deborah Blake

December 19
Thursday

4th ♏

☽ v/c 3:07 am

☽ → ♎ 5:04 am

Color of the Day: Crimson
Incense of the Day: Apricot

A Candle Flame Divination

Candles are used a great deal at this time of year for decorative purposes, but a candle flame can also be used to divine the future. For this ritual you'll need three white candles. They should be the same size and shape. Arrange them on a table or altar so they form a triangle. Light them safely.

Think of a yes-no question. Here's how you read the flames. If all the flames burn steadily, the answer is yes. If one flame sparks or goes out, you'll have an obstacle but you'll get what you want. If two or all the flames spark or go out, the answer is no. If all the flames sway or move in a circle, the answer hasn't been formed yet in the unseen realm. In this case, wait a few days and try again. When done, snuff out the candles.

James Kambos

December 20
Friday

4th ♎

Color of the Day: Rose
Incense of the Day: Orchid

Deep Dark Spell

Too often we are afraid of the dark, but as I tell my daughter, "There's nothing in the dark that isn't there in the light."

Tonight, claim the power of darkness. Walk slowly through your home, systematically turning off each light and saying:

What's in the light is all still here, so in the dark there's nothing to fear.

Turn off the last remaining light source and sit down. Sit with your fear or anxiety. Sit with it and breathe. Consciously slow down your breathing, and notice your heart rate responding and slowing. Be aware of your eyes adjusting to the dark as your pupils widen.

As you breathe and slow down, affirm and know:

What's in the light is all still here, so in the dark there's nothing to fear.

I am strong and capable, confident and brave.

I am at peace with the darkness, no longer afraid.

Dallas Jennifer Cobb

December 21
Saturday

4th ♎

☽ v/c 6:45 am

☽ → ♏ 7:57 am

☉ → ♑ 11:19 pm

Color of the Day: Gray
Incense of the Day: Patchouli

Yule – Winter Solstice

Sun Day, Sun Day!

A golden light rises in the sky, its light so bright that if you look directly into it, you'll be blinded. All life responds to its golden touch.

We call it our sun, but actually it's a ball of fire burning at more than 27 million degrees Fahrenheit. Thankfully its distance from Earth allows us to benefit from its immense heat, but stand in the sun's rays for too long and you'll surely get a sunburn (no matter your skin tone).

Appreciate the power of the sun, which we neither control nor command. Strike a yoga pose, or lift a burning sage bundle to our golden light.

Praise our sun:

Blessed orb of golden light,

Which lights our days and warms our nights,

Without you we could not be.

We honor you with love, respect, and humility.

Najah Lightfoot

December 22
Sunday

4th ♏︎

☽ v/c 10:27 pm

Color of the Day: Orange
Incense of the Day: Eucalyptus

Solstice Party Stone Soup

In the Northern Hemisphere this is one of the shortest days of the year, and it is hard to believe we are moving into more light. As a welcome to the holiday season and a celebration of more light, share a meal with family and friends. I am reminded of a particular book from my childhood called *Stone Soup*, in which villagers are tricked into providing ingredients for a pot of soup begun with water and a stone.

With or without a stone, add the ingredients for your favorite soup or stew. Invite family and friends. Add candles and/or firelight to welcome the longer days. Just for fun, obtain a copy of the book and read it aloud.

Chant:

Carrots, onions, potatoes, and beef,

*What more can we add to
make this complete?*

Stone at the bottom of this cooking pot,

Bring the magic, then let's eat!

Emyme

December 23
Monday

4th ♏︎

☽ → ♐︎ 11:34 am

Color of the Day: Gray
Incense of the Day: Narcissus

hanukkah begins (at sundown
on December 22)

Banishing Money Problems in the New Year

In just a few short days, 2019 will come to an end and soon we will all be gifted with another year of growth and abundance! Before we get there, though, there are likely a few energetic loose ends we should take care of, like making sure that any negative financial habits don't follow us into the new year. Cast this spell to do just that, and set yourself up for a truly prosperous 2020!

Mix together equal parts copal, sage, and eucalyptus incense and burn over a charcoal. Fumigate your home with the smoke, and as you do so, chant:

*I am prosperity. I am wishes
fulfilled and needs met. I am the
crown of success! I banish all
debt and financial devastation! It
shall not pass into the new year!
It shall have no place in my life!*

Seal the energy at the end by saying:

So mote it be!

Devin hunter

December 24
Tuesday

4♄ ♐

Color of the Day: Maroon
Incense of the Day: Cinnamon

Christmas Eve

The Sacred Pine

The pine tree and all the evergreens are at the center of many holiday celebrations. They are sacred symbols of eternal life, strength, hope, and wisdom. Let this spell inspire you now during the holiday season and beyond. You'll need some pine needles or a small pine branch, a heatproof container or a fireplace, and two pine cones. Place your pine needles or branch in the container or fireplace and light them. Hold the pine cones and pass them through the smoke. As you do this, say these Words of Power:

*Symbol of eternal life is
the mighty pine,*

*Standing tall and silent
since ancient times.*

*You who have seen the Ice Age
and the mountains rise,*

*Give me hope, give me strength,
and make me wise.*

The pine cones are now charged with the magical properties that the pines possess. Use these pine cones as a magical tool for spells dealing with strength, endurance, hope, or wisdom. You've also empowered your spirit. Wait until New Year's Day and scatter the pine ashes outside.

James Kambos

December 25
Wednesday

4th ♐

☽ v/c 6:18 am

☽ → ♑ 4:45 pm

Color of the Day: Topaz
Incense of the Day: Marjoram

Christmas Day

holly and Ivy Spell for Unity

Use the traditional holly and ivy plants for a spell to unite a partnership or friendship, or even to strengthen the bonds of family. Tie together a sprig of holly and ivy with a red ribbon. These plants have long been used in folklore for the winter holidays, so they should be easy to find. Holly is considered to have masculine energy and is associated with fire; ivy has feminine energy and is associated with water. Both have the qualities of protection and good fortune, and these two combined can represent balance and strength.

Speak these words as you place your holly and ivy bundle in a prominent place in your home:

*Bring us balance and
endurance of the evergreen,*

*With unity that no misfortune
can ever come between.*

Ember Grant

December 26
Thursday

4th ♑

☽ew Moon 12:13 am

Color of the Day: Green
Incense of the Day: Jasmine

Kwanzaa begins –
Boxing Day (Canada & UK) –
Solar Eclipse

Boxing Day: Know Your human Rights

The British Victorian tradition of the Christmas box is one of the first ways that aristocratic employers gave workers a holiday bonus, ensuring them a livable wage. As automation alters our labor model, the basic living wage is an increasingly popular subject on Boxing Day. What is our own evolution of rudimentary human rights? Are we living on outdated and unhealthy commodities? Take stock of our shared birthright to the earth's sustainable resources.

Our allotment of food, shelter, medicine, and goods—if assured— is only for right now; our very next moment brings with it constant change. Gather with family to discuss ways to positively impact those places in the community where environmental, labor, or civil rights are under threat; the struggle may be closer to home than you think.

Finally, work together to craft a

care package and gift it to someone who has worked tirelessly and is in need of sustainability on this day of reflection and gratitude.

Estha McNevin

NOTES:

December 27
Friday

1st ♑

☽ v/c 4:03 pm

Color of the Day: Purple
Incense of the Day: Yarrow

Do We have to Be Serious All the Time?

Back in the Middle Ages at the tail end of the year, the Feast of Fools (with temporary reversals of status) was celebrated. What can we do today? Our magic doesn't always have to be Highly Serious.

First, go to a toy store and buy some wind-up toys—witches, frogs, little airplanes, anything that moves. Cast your circle and skew the altar a bit so the sylphs, undines, salamanders, and gnomes get some new scenery. Set toys or Muppets in the four directions:

Air: Sam the Eagle

Fire: Animal

Water: Kermit the Frog

Earth: Miss Piggy

In the center, place a toy Christmas tree decorated with pastel Cheerios (the year goes round and round).

Instead of the usual invocations, sing old folk songs or disco songs.

Don't light candles. That's too dangerous when you wind up all the toys and set them loose on the altar.

Barbara Ardinger

December 28
Saturday

1st ♑

☽ → ♒ 12:21 am

Color of the Day: Indigo
Incense of the Day: Pine

You're a Superhero!

Today is the birthday of Stan Lee, comic book writer, editor, and publisher extraordinaire! Stan has brought us many beloved superheroes. While comic book heroes inspire us, it's important to remember that we too can be inspiring with the gifts we have to offer the world.

Today, light a white, gold, or yellow candle in a holder upon your altar. Think about all the ways in which you use your gifts and abilities to help others. Write them down in a list on a small piece of paper. Then fold the list and place it under the holder as the candle burns down. While looking at the candle, visualize melding with the power of its light as you begin to glow with power. Visualize yourself glowing radiantly with your own power, the power you use to do good in the world with your gifts. When the candle burns out, you can carry the list as a reminder when needed.

Blake Octavian Blair

December 29
Sunday

1st ≈

Color of the Day: Gold
Incense of the Day: Almond

Stringing Up Abundance

People most often think of making decorative strings for Yule or Christmas, but afterward these strings take on a different tone. Now is a good time to make decorations for your upcoming New Year festivities. Don't leave it until the last minute, because these take time.

This spell simply involves concentrating on prosperity while you string up symbols of abundance.

Popcorn is traditional, as corn is a very fecund grain. Also, after you're done hanging it around your house, you can move it outside for wildlife to enjoy.

Nuts serve a similar purpose. Peanuts may be sewn through the shell. Most other nuts must be glued on or knotted into a net.

Coins are ideal for representing prosperity. You can string gold plastic coins, but real pennies work better. Glue them in a sandwich around monofilament line. You can do the same with tiny mirrors to vary the display.

Elizabeth Barrette

December 30
Monday

1st ≈

☽ v/c 5:24 am
☽ → ♓ 10:41 am

Color of the Day: Ivory
Incense of the Day: Hyssop

hanukkah ends

Fire and Water Fortunetelling

For this divination you will need a purple votive candle and a bowl of cold water (melted snow or rain if possible).

Light the candle, and as it burns, think about a question or issue for which you would like an answer. If you don't have a specific query, you can ask, *What influences are entering my life now?*

Once the top of the votive candle has accumulated a substantial puddle of wax without spilling over, carefully dump the wax into the water all at once. When it cools, take the wax out of the water and flip it over. It will have solidified into interesting shapes as it hit the cold water.

What do the wax lumps and bumps look like? You may see animals, objects, or faces. How do you decide what they mean? The first feeling or association that pops into your head is usually the answer. Write down your impressions so you can revisit them later.

Kate Freuler

December 31

Tuesday

1st ♓

Color of the Day: White

Incense of the Day: Basil

New Year's Eve

New Year Lemon Charm

Inspired by Leland's *Aradia*, this spell can be used to bless the home for the coming year. It is appropriate to make this charm to give as a gift, for to receive one in such a manner is said to bring the added blessing of a prosperous and joyful life. You will need:

- 3 lengths of ribbon: green, purple, and red
- Several pins with colored heads (except for black)
- A lemon

Braid the ribbons together, saying:

Health and power,

Prosperity,

Love, sex, and creativity.

Repeat the chant until you have finished your braid. Now stick the pins into the lemon until it is entirely covered with an array of colored pins.

Attach the braid to the lemon so that it may be hung in the home. When it is hung (preferably at midnight), say:

As midnight strikes its final chime,

The power of this spell unfolds.

Abundant blessings, all sublime,

Upon this house are now bestowed.

Storm Faerywolf

Daily Magical Influences

Each day is ruled by a planet that pxossesses specific magical influences:

Monday (Moon): peace, healing, caring, psychic awareness, purification.

Tuesday (Mars): passion, sex, courage, aggression, protection.

Wednesday (Mercury): conscious mind, study, travel, divination, wisdom.

Thursday (Jupiter): expansion, money, prosperity, generosity.

Friday (Venus): love, friendship, reconciliation, beauty.

Saturday (Saturn): longevity, exorcism, endings, homes, houses.

Sunday (Sun): healing, spirituality, success, strength, protection.

Lunar Phases

The lunar phase is important in determining best times for magic.

The waxing moon (from the new moon to the full moon) is the ideal time for magic to draw things toward you.

The full moon is the time of greatest power.

The waning moon (from the full moon to the new moon) is a time for study, meditation, and little magical work (except magic designed to banish harmful energies).

Astrological Symbols

The Sun	☉	Aries	♈
The Moon	☽	Taurus	♉
Mercury	☿	Gemini	♊
Venus	♀	Cancer	♋
Mars	♂	Leo	♌
Jupiter	♃	Virgo	♍
Saturn	♄	Libra	♎
Uranus	♅	Scorpio	♏
Neptune	♆	Sagittarius	♐
Pluto	♇	Capricorn	♑
		Aquarius	♒
		Pisces	♓

The Moon's Sign

The moon's sign is a traditional consideration for astrologers. The moon continuously moves through each sign in the zodiac, from Aries to Pisces. The moon influences the sign it inhabits, creating different energies that affect our daily lives.

Aries: Good for starting things but lacks staying power. Things occur rapidly but quickly pass. People tend to be argumentative and assertive.

Taurus: Things begun now do last, tend to increase in value, and become hard to alter. Brings out an appreciation for beauty and sensory experience.

Gemini: Things begun now are easily changed by outside influence. Time for shortcuts, communications, games, and fun.

Cancer: Stimulates emotional rapport between people. Pinpoints need, supports growth and nurturance. Tend to domestic concerns.

Leo: Draws emphasis to the self, to central ideas or institutions, away from connections with others and emotional needs. People tend to be melodramatic.

Virgo: Favors accomplishment of details and commands from higher up. Focus on health, hygiene, and daily schedules.

Libra: Favors cooperation, compromise, social activities, beautification of surroundings, balance, and partnership.

Scorpio: Increases awareness of psychic power. Favors activities requiring intensity and focus. People tend to brood and become secretive under this moon sign.

Sagittarius: Encourages flights of imagination and confidence. This moon sign is adventurous, philosophical, and athletic. Favors expansion and growth.

Capricorn: Develops strong structure. Focus on traditions, responsibilities, and obligations. A good time to set boundaries and rules.

Aquarius: Rebellious energy. Time to break habits and make abrupt change. Personal freedom and individuality are the focus.

Pisces: The focus is on dreaming, nostalgia, intuition, and psychic impressions. A good time for spiritual or philanthropic activities.

Glossary of Magical Terms

Altar: A table that holds magical tools as a focus for spell workings.

Athame: A ritual knife used to direct personal power during workings or to symbolically draw diagrams in a spell. It is rarely, if ever, used for actual physical cutting.

Aura: An invisible energy field surrounding a person. The aura can change color depending on the state of the individual.

Balefire: A fire lit for magical purposes, usually outdoors.

Casting a circle: The process of drawing a circle around oneself to seal out unfriendly influences and raise magical power. It is the first step in a spell.

Censer: An incense burner. Traditionally a censer is a metal container, filled with incense, that is swung on the end of a chain.

Censing: The process of burning incense to spiritually cleanse an object.

Centering yourself: To prepare for a magical rite by calming and centering all of your personal energy.

Chakra: One of the seven centers of spiritual energy in the human body, according to the philosophy of yoga.

Charging: To infuse an object with magical power.

Circle of protection: A circle cast to protect oneself from unfriendly influences.

Crystals: Quartz or other stones that store cleansing or protective energies.

Deosil: Clockwise movement, symbolic of life and positive energies.

Deva: A divine being according to Hindu beliefs; a devil or evil spirit according to Zoroastrianism.

Direct/retrograde: Refers to the motion of a planet when seen from the earth. A planet is "direct" when it appears to be moving forward from the point of view of a person on the earth. It is "retrograde" when it appears to be moving backward.

Dowsing: To use a divining rod to search for a thing, usually water or minerals.

Dowsing pendulum: A long cord with a coin or gem at one end. The pattern of its swing is used to answer questions.

Dryad: A tree spirit or forest guardian.

Fey: An archaic term for a magical spirit or a fairylike being.

Gris-gris: A small bag containing charms, herbs, stones, and other items to draw energy, luck, love, or prosperity to the wearer.

Mantra: A sacred chant used in Hindu tradition to embody the divinity invoked; it is said to possess deep magical power.

Needfire: A ceremonial fire kindled at dawn on major Wiccan holidays. It was traditionally used to light all other household fires.

Pentagram: A symbolically protective five-pointed star with one point upward.

Power hand: The dominant hand; the hand used most often.

Scry: To predict the future by gazing at or into an object such as a crystal ball or pool of water.

Second sight: The psychic power or ability to foresee the future.

Sigil: A personal seal or symbol.

Smudge/smudge stick: To spiritually cleanse an object by waving smoke over and around it. A smudge stick is a bundle of several incense sticks.

Wand: A stick or rod used for casting circles and as a focus for magical power.

Widdershins: Counterclockwise movement, symbolic of negative magical purposes, sometimes used to disperse negative energies.

About the Authors

Barbara Ardinger, PhD (www.barbaraardinger.com, www.facebook.com /barbara.ardinger), is the author of *Secret Lives*, a novel about a circle of crones, mothers, and maidens, plus goddesses, a talking cat, and the Green Man. Her earlier books include the daybook *Pagan Every Day*, *Goddess Meditations*, *Finding New Goddesses* (a parody of goddess encyclopedias), and *Quicksilver Moon* (a realistic novel…except for the vampire). She is also well known for the rituals she creates. Her day job is freelance editing for people who have good ideas but don't want to embarrass themselves in print. Barbara lives in Southern California with her two rescued Maine coon cats, Heisenberg and Schroedinger.

Elizabeth Barrette has been involved with the Pagan community for more than twenty-eight years. She served as managing editor of *PanGaia* for eight years and dean of studies at the Grey School of Wizardry for four years. She has written columns on beginning and intermediate Pagan practice, Pagan culture, and Pagan leadership. Her book *Composing Magic: How to Create Magical Spells, Rituals, Blessings, Chants, and Prayers* explains how to combine writing and spirituality. She lives in central Illinois, where she has done much networking with Pagans in her area, such as coffeehouse meetings and open sabbats. Her other public activities include Pagan picnics and science fiction conventions. She enjoys magical crafts, historical religions, and gardening for wildlife. Her other writing fields include speculative fiction, gender studies, and social and environmental issues. Visit her blog, *The Wordsmith's Forge*, at https://ysabetwordsmith.livejournal.com.

Stephanie Rose Bird is a Chicago-area artist, writer, and published author, specializing in alternative spiritually and Hoodoo. She's had six books published: *Earth Mama's Spiritual Guide to Weight Loss; The Big Book of Soul; A Healing Grove; Light, Bright, and Damned Near White; Sticks, Stones, Roots & Bones;* and *Four Seasons of Mojo*. Her seventh book, *365 Days of Hoodoo*, will be published in 2019 by Llewellyn. Her first book, *Sticks, Stones, Roots & Bones*, won a COVR Award. For more, visit her website at www.stephanierosebird.com.

Blake Octavian Blair is a shamanic practitioner, ordained minister, writer, Usui Reiki Master-Teacher, tarot reader, and musical artist. Blake incorporates mystical traditions from both the East and the West, along with a reverence for the natural world, into his own brand of spirituality. Blake holds a degree in English and Religion from the University of Florida. He is an avid reader, knitter, crafter, pescatarian, and member of the Order of Bards, Ovates, and Druids (OBOD). He loves communing with nature and exploring its beauty. Blake lives in the New England region of the US with his beloved husband. Visit him on the web at www.blakeoctavianblair.com or write to him at blake@blakeoctavianblair.com.

Deborah Blake is the award-winning author of the Baba Yaga and Broken Rider paranormal romance series and the Veiled Magic urban fantasies from Berkley. Deborah has also written *The Goddess Is in the Details*, *Everyday Witchcraft*, and numerous other books from Llewellyn, along with a popular tarot deck. She has published articles in Llewellyn annuals, and her ongoing column, "Everyday Witchcraft," is featured in *Witches & Pagans* magazine. Deborah can be found online at Facebook, Twitter, her popular blog (*Writing the Witchy Way*), and www.deborahblakeauthor.com. She lives in a 130-year-old farmhouse in rural upstate New York with various cats who supervise all her activities, both magickal and mundane.

Dallas Jennifer Cobb practices gratitude magic, giving thanks for ongoing healing, wholeness, and prosperity, a variety of flexible and rewarding work, and quiet contentment. She lives with her daughter in paradise—a waterfront village in rural Ontario, where she regularly swims, hikes, meditates, and snowshoes. A Reclaiming witch from way back, Jennifer is part of an eclectic pan-Pagan circle that organizes magical and empowering community rituals. Contact her at jennifer.cobb@live.com.

Emyme is a solitary eclectic who resides in southern New Jersey with her beloved cats and specializes in candle and garden spells and kitchen witchery. Apart from her full-time job out in the world, she writes poetry about strong women of mythology and flash fiction with a modern twist on traditional fairy tales. Emyme is looking forward to retirement and the opportunity to devote more time to her craft and her writing, and to the fresh challenge of moving from Mother to Crone status. Please send questions or comments to catsmeow24@verizon.net.

Storm Faerywolf is a published author, experienced teacher, visionary artist, and professional warlock. He inherits the Old Craft by way of the Faery tradition, where he holds the Black Wand of a Master. He is the author of *Betwixt and Between: Exploring the Faery Tradition of Witchcraft* and *The Stars Within the Earth*. He travels internationally teaching and lecturing on magic and the Craft, but makes his home in the San Francisco Bay area

with his loving partners and a menagerie of very spoiled animal companions. For more, visit his website at faerywolf.com.

Kate Freuler lives in Ontario, Canada, with her husband and daughter. She owns and operates www.whitemoonwitchcraft.com, an online witchcraft boutique. When she isn't crafting spells and amulets for clients or herself, she loves to write, paint, read, draw, and create.

Ember Grant has been writing for the Llewellyn annuals since 2003 and is the author of three books: *Magical Candle Crafting*, *The Book of Crystal Spells*, and *The Second Book of Crystal Spells*. She lives in Missouri with her husband and two feline companions. Visit her at EmberGrant.com.

Devin Hunter (San Francisco Bay Area) is a bestselling author who holds initiations in multiple spiritual, occult, and esoteric traditions and is the founder of his own tradition, Sacred Fires, and co-founder of its offshoot community, Black Rose Witchcraft. His podcast, *The Modern Witch*, has helped thousands of people from all over the world empower themselves and discover their psychic and magical abilities. Devin is the co-owner of the Mystic Dream, a metaphysical store in Walnut Creek, CA, where he offers professional services as a medium and occultist.

James Kambos is a regular contributor to the Llewellyn annuals. He has a degree in history and geography. When not writing, he's an artist and he designs cards.

Najah Lightfoot is a writer and contributor for Llewellyn Publications. She is a sister-priestess of the Divine Feminine, a martial artist, and an active member of the Denver Pagan community. She keeps her magick strong through the indigenous practices of her ancestors, the folk magick of Hoodoo, Pagan rituals, and her belief in the mysteries of the universe. She finds inspiration in movies, music, and the blue skies of Colorado. Find her online at www.twitter.com/NajahLightfoot, www.facebook.com/NajahLightfoot, and www.craftandconjure.com.

Melanie Marquis is the creator of the *Modern Spellcaster's Tarot* (illustrated by Scott Murphy) and the author of several books, including *A Witch's World of Magick*; *The Witch's Bag of Tricks*; *Carl Llewellyn Weschcke: Pioneer and Publisher of Body, Mind & Spirit*; *Witchy Mama* (with Emily A. Francis); *Beltane*; and *Lughnasadh*. The founder of United Witches Global Coven and a local coordinator for the Pagan Pride Project, she loves sharing magick with others and has presented workshops and rituals to audiences across the US. She lives in Denver, Colorado.

Estha McNevin (Missoula, MT) is a Priestess and ceremonial oracle of Opus Aima Obscuræ, a nonprofit Pagan temple haus. She has served the Pagan community since 2003 as an Eastern Hellenistic officiate, lecturer, freelance author, artist, and poet. Estha studies and teaches courses on ancient and modern Pagan history. She offers classes on multicultural metaphysical theory, ritual technique, international cuisine, organic gardening, herbal craft, alchemy, and occult symbolism. In addition to hosting public rituals for the sabbats, Estha organizes annual philanthropic fundraisers, full moon spellcrafting ceremonies, and women's divination rituals for each dark moon. To learn more, please explore www.facebook.com/opusaimaobscurae.

Spell Notes

Spell Notes

Spell Notes

Spell Notes

Llewellyn's 2019 Witches' Calendar

Since 1998, *Llewellyn's Witches' Calendar* has been a favorite way to mark the turning of the Wheel of the Year. This beautiful calendar features magical wisdom, astrological data, and Witch's holidays, making it the perfect choice for bringing more happiness and enchantment into your year.

Each month features a beautiful, original scratchboard illustration by award-winning artist Kathleen Edwards as well as an inspiring article and spell or ritual. Discover a May flower spell for rebirth, a personal ritual for shadow work, a prosperity spell for the holiday season, how to perform bibliomancy, how to employ gnomes as home guardians, and more. Magical correspondences are also included.

978-0-7387-4614-2, 28 pp., 12 x 12 $14.99

To order, call 1-877-NEW-WRLD or visit llewellyn.com
Prices subject to change without notice

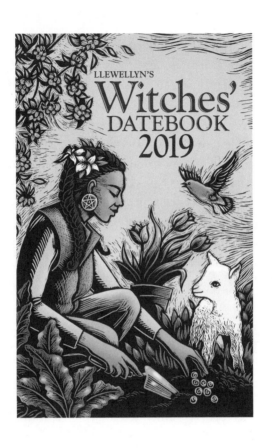

LLEWELLYN'S

Witches'
DATEBOOK
2019

Llewellyn's 2019 Witches' Datebook

Live your craft throughout the year and stay organized while you do it. *Llewellyn's 2019 Witches' Datebook* features beautiful illustrations from award-winning artist Kathleen Edwards, a variety of ways to celebrate the Wheel of the Year, and powerful wisdom from practicing Witches.

Find fresh ways to celebrate the sacred seasons and enhance your practice with sabbat musings (Raven Digitalis), tasty sabbat recipes (Estha McNevin), witchy tips (Elizabeth Barrette), and the Witch's tools (Mickie Mueller). Also included are fascinating articles on connecting magically with birds (Monica Crosson), prioritizing spells and rituals (Diana Rajchel), ethically disposing of offering items (Blake Octavian Blair), visualizing with all five senses (Autumn Damiana), and changing your body to match the energy of your goal (Charlynn Walls). This indispensable, on-the-go tool will make all your days more magical.

978-0-7387-4616-6, 168 pp., 5 ¼ x 8 $12.99

GET MORE AT LLEWELLYN.COM

Visit us online to browse hundreds of our books and decks, plus sign up to receive our e-newsletters and exclusive online offers.

- **Free tarot readings • Spell-a-Day • Moon phases**
- **Recipes, spells, and tips • Blogs • Encyclopedia**
- **Author interviews, articles, and upcoming events**

GET SOCIAL WITH LLEWELLYN

Find us on  **@LlewellynBooks**

www.Facebook.com/LlewellynBooks

GET BOOKS AT LLEWELLYN

LLEWELLYN ORDERING INFORMATION

Order online: Visit our website at www.llewellyn.com to select your books and place an order on our secure server.

Order by phone:
- Call toll free within the US at 1-877-NEW-WRLD (1-877-639-9753)
- We accept VISA, MasterCard, American Express, and Discover.
- Canadian customers must use credit cards.

Order by mail:
Send the full price of your order (MN residents add 6.875% sales tax) in US funds plus postage and handling to: Llewellyn Worldwide, 2143 Wooddale Drive, Woodbury, MN 55125-2989

POSTAGE AND HANDLING
STANDARD (US):
(Please allow 12 business days)
$30.00 and under, add $6.00.
$30.01 and over, FREE SHIPPING.

INTERNATIONAL ORDERS,
INCLUDING CANADA:
$16.00 for one book, plus $3.00 for each additional book.

Visit us online for more shipping options.
Prices subject to change.

FREE CATALOG!

To order, call
1-877-
NEW-WRLD
ext. 8236
or visit our
website